Mets
Triviology

Christopher Walsh

TRIUMPH
BOOKS

Library of Congress Cataloging-in-Publication Data

Names: Walsh, Christopher.
Title: Mets triviology : fascinating facts from the bleacher seats / Christopher Walsh.
Description: Chicago, Illinois : Triumph Books, [2016]
Identifiers: LCCN 2016001671
Subjects: LCSH: New York Mets (Baseball team)—Miscellanea.
Classification: LCC GV875.N45 W35 2016 | DDC 796.357/64097471—dc23 LC record available at http://lccn.loc.gov/2016001671

This book is available in quantity at special discounts for your group or organization. For further information, contact:

Triumph Books LLC
814 North Franklin Street
Chicago, Illinois 60610
(312) 676-4247
www.triumphbooks.com

Printed in U.S.A.
ISBN: 978-1-62937-236-5
Design by Meghan Grammer
All photos are courtesy of AP Images.

SPECIAL THANKS
To Noah Amstadter, Tom Bast, Jesse Jordan and everyone else at Triumph Books who worked on this project.

For Mets fans everywhere, especially the ones I went to school with at the University of New Hampshire.

"I just want to taste what it's like to win in New York."
—*David Wright*

Contents

Introduction

It was the fall of 1986 and I was a freshman the University of New Hampshire. I had grown up a sports nut, but nothing quite prepared me for those first couple of months on campus when the New York Mets and the Boston Red Sox were on a collision course to meet in the World Series and the whole region went nuts.

I mean really, really nuts, which was fitting considering the way things played out on the diamond, yet that was my first taste of what people meant when they said that Boston and New York were baseball cities. With each big victory, impromptu victory celebrations broke out and lasted well into the morning hours.

Two friends down the hall had a TV and we'd all cram into their room to watch every game, with those rooting for the Red Sox on one side and the Mets fans on the other (being the "foreigner" from Minnesota I sat in the middle). When the ball went between Bill Buckner's legs in Game 6 everyone screamed, some in joy, others in absolute horror. My roommate who had been making plans to celebrate the victory froze and sat in shock staring at the screen for about 90 minutes after we turned both it and the lights off.

Years later I got a second, even stronger taste when I was a sportswriter based in Phoenix and the Arizona Diamondbacks faced the New York Mets during their first appearance in the playoffs. Buck

Showalter, then the manager of the Diamondbacks, once said to me, "New York is a special place in October when the teams are in the playoffs," and it certainly was, but not for his team.

After losing Game 1, Showalter rolled the dice a little and held Cy Young winner Randy Johnson for a potential Game 5, which gave Game 4 a definite must-win feeling for the Mets at Shea Stadium. Because his bullpen had been sketchy in the series he brought in closer Matt Mantei as part of a double move with one out in the eighth (taking out third baseman Matt Williams, which raised more than a few eyebrows in the press box).

The inning ended with the Mets having tied the score 3–3, and Mantei stayed in the game not only through the ninth, but into the 10th when backup catcher Todd Pratt hit a long fly ball to center field just beyond Steve Finley's reach for the game-winning home run. I'm still not sure how the stadium remained standing following the emotional explosion that was like nothing I had ever experienced before.

That's what the Mets taught me over the years, what October baseball was really all about, and how wonderful it could be.

Hopefully some of that will come through in the pages to follow.

In putting this book together my aim wasn't to be overly easy or difficult, or have it serve as a quiz to measure the baseball IQ of even the most die-hard fans, but rather to celebrate, honor, and inform. The Mets are one of the most interesting and colorful franchises to have ever existed, and it's hard to believe sometimes that they've only been around since the 1960s.

The book is organized into sections to make it easy to use and at times it breaks down into subsections. The questions range in difficulty from "No, duh" to extremely difficult, and those in the Hot Box section are practically impossible.

Above all else, I hope you enjoy it and learn a few things along the way.

One

The Basics

It began not just with something lost, but also the notion that New York needed to have more than just one Major League Baseball team (or as some would put it an alternative to that team in pinstripes). With the Dodgers and Giants moving to the West Coast, which just never felt right in a city that prided itself on fierce allegiances and loyalties that transcended territories and families, what they left behind was more than a bad aftertaste, but a burning desire to reclaim something that had been taken from them.

Thus was the essence of the subsequent threat, because that's what attorney William Shea did in response, threaten Major League Baseball to its core by announcing in 1959 the formation of a third major league. The Continental League would begin play two years later and one of the charter teams would be placed in New York.

A year later the league disbanded, but out of it the New York Metropolitan Baseball Club Inc. became an expansion franchise on March 6, 1961. After the conclusion of the subsequent season the first expansion draft in National League history was held on October 10 at the Netherland-Hilton Hotel in Cincinnati.

The new team spent $1.8 million to select 22 players and 18 days later construction crews broke ground on building a new stadium.

Also unveiled in November 1961 was the circular Mets logo, which has virtually remained unchanged. The circular shape obviously represents a baseball, and the bridge in the foreground symbolizes the National League returning to New York.

According to the Mets' media guide the skyline also has special meaning: At the left is a church spire, symbolic of Brooklyn, the borough of churches. The second building from the left is the Williamsburg Savings Bank, the tallest building in Brooklyn. Next is the Woolworth Building. After a general skyline view of midtown comes the Empire State Building. At the far right is the United Nations Building.

The Basics

1.   Why were the Mets said to be wearing "copycat" uniforms?
2.   The Mets' colors are also the official colors of what else?
3.   Who designed the Mets' logo?
4.   Which former minority owner of the Giants, who voted against the franchise's move to San Francisco, was the Mets' first owner?
5.   Who was the first team president and hired Casey Stengel to be the team's first manager?
6.   Who was the first player the Mets took in the expansion draft?
7.   What happened on April 10, 1962, when the new franchise was set to play its first regular-season game?
8.   What other anomaly occurred during the Mets' first home game at the Polo Grounds?
9.   What did it take for the Mets to win their first game on April 23, 1962?
10. What lengthy streak did that same player help end later in the season? (Hint: It was a franchise record that still stands)
11. What did the Mets do for the first of 1,859 times on April 19, 1964?
12. What did Shea Stadium host only once, on July 7, 1964?

13. Between November 17–23, 1964, what two future Hall of Fame players did the Mets sign?
14. What three well-known Mets broadcasters worked together for 17 years?
15. Who notched his first win in the Major Leagues on April 14, 1968?
16. What supposedly brought the Mets good luck during the 1969 pennant chase?
17. What did the Mets host for the first time on October 14, 1969?
18. Who threw the strikeout to clinch the 1986 World Series?
19. What was the outcome of the 2000 Subway Series?
20. Who hit a two-run home run in the eighth inning to lead a 3–2 victory over the Atlanta Braves in New York City's first sporting event after the tragic events of September 11th?

Maintenance crews work on March 29, 1962, to prepare the Polo Grounds for the inaugural season of the New York Mets.

Answers

1. The Mets' colors are Dodger blue and Giant orange, "symbolic of the return of National League baseball to New York after the Dodgers and Giants moved to California."
2. New York State
3. Sports cartoonist Ray Gatto.
4. Joan Whitney Payson
5. George Weiss. He was elected to the Baseball Hall of Fame in 1971.
6. Hobie Landrith
7. The game was rained out.
8. It snowed. Attendance was only 12,447.
9. A 5-hitter from Jay Hook.
10. Jay Hooks led a 4–3 victory over the Cubs to snap a 17-game losing streak, the longest in franchise history.
11. Win at Shea Stadium, the team's new home.
12. The All-Star Game
13. Yogi Berra and Warren Spahn
14. Ralph Kiner, Bob Murphy, and Lindsey Nelson.
15. Nolan Ryan
16. A black cat. It emerged in front of the Cubs dugout at Shea Stadium and stared at the visiting players. The Mets won 7–1.
17. A World Series game
18. Jesse Orosco
19. The Yankees beat the Mets in five games.
20. Mike Piazza

Two

National League History

Although the New York Mets didn't join the National League until the 1962 season, its roots go back to 1876.

To put that into perspective it's the year Colorado became the 38th state, General George Armstrong Custer was killed along with 264 of his Union Calvary after engaging the Sioux tribe at Little Big Horn, and Thomas Edison had yet to invent the light bulb.

The idea of professional baseball was a few years old, but the National Association of Professional Base Ball Players was anything but stable and was dominated by one team, the Boston Red Stockings.

In part because five of his star players were on the verge of being kicked out of the league, Chicago businessman William Hulbert started rallying support for the creation of a new league, which became the National League.

The reason why it's called the Senior Circuit is that it was around 25 years before the American League, which for a while it considered an inferior league.

National League History

1. What was the original name of the National League?
2. Name the original eight teams.
3. Which two still exist?
4. Which two organizations were kicked out of the league during the first year, and why?
5. What happened to the other four teams that are no longer in existence?
6. Which two teams that are still in the National League joined in 1883?
7. Where was the first National League game played?
8. How many games was each team scheduled to play that season?
9. Who had the first hit in National League history?
10. Who is credited with scoring the first run?
11. Who had both the first double and triple?
12. Who had the first home run?
13. Who threw the first no-hitter?
14. What major innovation occurred in 1877?
15. Although many upstart leagues would challenge the National League, which was its first significant rival?
16. Which four teams switched allegiances and joined the National League prior to 1892?
17. When the two leagues essentially merged which four franchises joined the National League in 1892?
18. Which one of those four continues to exist today?
19. When was the first modern World Series played and who won?
20. After the National League existed as an eight-team league for more than 50 years, which expansion team joined along with the New York Mets in 1962?

Answers

1. The National League of Professional Baseball
2. The Boston Red Stockings, Chicago White Stockings, Cincinnati Red Legs, Hartford Dark Blues, Louisville Grays, Philadelphia Athletics, Brooklyn Mutuals and St. Louis Browns
3. The Boston Red Stockings are now the Atlanta Braves, and the Chicago White Stockings became the Chicago Cubs. It's the only original team that never moved.
4. After falling behind in the standings the Athletics and Mutuals refused to make western road trips late in the season, opting to instead play local teams to save money. Hulbert expelled them.
5. Three of them folded within two years. The Cincinnati Red Stockings were expelled after the 1880 season.
6. The New York Gothams and Philadelphia Phillies. The Gothams are now known as the San Francisco Giants.
7. Philadelphia's Jefferson Street Grounds, 25th & Jefferson. Boston defeated the hometown team 6–5.
8. 70
9. Jim O'Rourke
10. Tim McGinley
11. Levi Meyerle
12. Chicago's Ross Barnes. Cincinnati's William "Cherokee" Fisher was the pitcher.
13. St. Louis' George Bradley, against Hartford.
14. Al Spalding made the first major league baseball glove.
15. The American Association
16. The teams now known as the Cincinnati Reds, Los Angeles Dodgers, Pittsburgh Pirates, and the now-defunct Cleveland Spiders.
17. The Baltimore Orioles, Louisville Colonels, St. Louis Perfectos, and the Washington Senators.
18. The St. Louis Perfectos, which became the St. Louis Cardinals. The other three were contracted after the 1899 season. The team now called the Baltimore Orioles were the St. Louis Browns, who moved in 1953.
19. 1903, the Boston Americans of the American League faced the Pittsburgh Pirates of the National League in a best-of-nine series. Boston won the last four games to win the series 5–3.
20. The Houston Colt .45s, who were renamed the Astros in 1965.

Three

Famous Firsts

Although the New York Mets have had many illustrious firsts along the way, one that some believed might never happen was the first no-hitter.

It took 50 seasons and 8,020 games before a Mets pitcher was finally able to come through.

Johan Santana, who had won two Cy Young Awards with the Minnesota Twins, was the pitcher to make history during the Mets' 8–0 victory over the St. Louis Cardinals at Citi Field on June 1, 2012.

Like with most no-hitters his had a fair share of near-miss plays, like a foul ball call on a Carlos Beltran line drive over third base that appeared to land on the chalk line (he subsequently grounded out to third baseman David Wright) and left fielder Mike Baxter's seventh-inning catch to rob Yadier Molina of a possible extra-base hit.

"Every pitcher wants to do it at least one time," Santana told *Sports Illustrated* in 2015. "There's something about it, the way you never see it coming. Once you start to get close, can you make the pitches you need to finish it? But mostly it's the surprise. The surprise makes it special."

However, the left-hander needed 134 pitches to get through the game against the reigning world champions and was arguably never the same again. It was just his 11th start after having shoulder surgery and Santana re-tore his shoulder before the start of the 2013 season.

Terry Collins hugs Johan Santana after Santana's no-hitter against the Cardinals on June 1, 2012. (Kathy Kmonicek)

Famous Firsts

1. Who was the first batter in franchise history?
2. Who had the first RBI?
3. What franchise first occurred to the Mets on May 30, 1962, during the second game of a doubleheader against the Dodgers at the Polo Grounds? (Bonus: Name the batter.)
4. Who hit the first home run in franchise history?
5. Who hit the first inside-the-park home run in franchise history?
6. What was the Mets' record during their first season?
7. In what year did the Mets win their first season opener?
8. Who was the first pitcher in franchise history to throw back-to-back shutouts?
9. Who was the first player in Mets history to hit for the cycle?
10. Who was the first opposing player to hit for the cycle against the Mets?
11. Who threw the first no-hitter against the Mets?
12. Who was the first Met to have a 100-RBI season?
13. Who was the first player in franchise history to hit a home run during his first Major League at-bat?
14. Who was the first player in Mets history to hit a home run off the first pitch he saw in the majors?
15. On July 10, 1963, the Mets lost their first 1–0 game that was decided by a home run. Who was the pitcher? (Bonus: Name the batter.)
16. On June 14, 1965, the Mets won their first game by a 1–0 score with the lone run coming off a home run. Who hit it?
17. Who won the first Gold Glove Award in Mets history?
18. Who is the only player in franchise history to hit two inside-the-park home runs during the same season?
19. Who was the first winner of the John J. Murphy Award for the top Met rookie in spring training?

20. Which person not technically in the organization won the award in 2000?
21. Who was the first Mets pitcher to strike out four batters in an inning?
22. Who had the first jersey number retired by the Mets?
23. Who made the final out for the Cardinals in Santana's no-hitter?
24. How was he retired?
25. How many times had a Mets pitcher come within an out of throwing a no-hitter before the franchise finally celebrated one?

Answers

1. Richie Ashburn, who flew out to center field against the St. Louis Cardinals. Incidentally, Larry Jackson threw the pitch and Curt Flood recorded the out.
2. Charlie Neal, who hit a single to score Richie Ashburn in the third inning.
3. The first triple play, Willie Davis was the batter.
4. Gil Hodges
5. Gil Hodges
6. 40–122, to finish 60½ games out of first place in the standings.
7. 1970, after losing the first eight.
8. Jerry Koosman in 1968. On April 11 he topped the Dodgers 4–0, and on the 17ᵗʰ beat the Giants 3–0.
9. Jim Hickman on August 7, 1963, against the St. Louis Cardinals.
10. Wes Parker of the Los Angeles Dodgers on May 7, 1990.
11. Sandy Koufax, 5–0 on June 30, 1962.
12. Rusty Staub in 1975.
13. Benny Ayala on August 27, 1974.
14. Mike Bordick on July 29, 2000.
15. Carl Willey. The home run was hit by the Dodgers' Johnny Roseboro.
16. Johnny Lewis at Cincinnati.
17. Outfielder Tommy Agee in 1970.
18. Actually, it's never been done (at least when this book was published). Darryl Strawberry is the only one who has more than one with the Mets.
19. John Milner in 1972.
20. Garth Brooks
21. Derek Wallace on September 13, 1996, vs. Atlanta.
22. Casey Stengel's 37
23. David Freese
24. He struck out after getting ahead in the count 3–0.
25. 35.

Four

The Stadiums

Although Citi Field didn't host its first game until 2009 the stadium had been years in the making as the Mets started looking to replace outdated Shea Stadium as early as the 1990s.

In 1998 it unveiled a preliminary model of a new ballpark featuring a retractable roof and a movable grass field, which would have allowed it to host events including conventions and college basketball. Numerous sites were considered, including West Side Yard in Manhattan, Sunnyside Yard in Queens, and multiple locations in Long Island, but it ended up being built next door to the structure it replaced, Shea Stadium.

Just how the deal got done and the contracts all signed was nothing short of a drawn-out dizzying experience that took years to complete. Here's the super-short version:

Shortly before leaving office, New York City Mayor Rudy Giuliani announced in December 2001 "tentative agreements" for both the Mets and New York Yankees to build new stadiums. However it was widely criticized due to taxpayers being on the hook for more than $800 million for construction and $390 million for extra transportation.

Guiliani's successor Michael Bloomberg exercised the escape clause to back out of both deals, saying that the city could not afford to build new stadiums, only to trigger another proviso allowing the teams to relocate on just 60 days' notice.

Meanwhile, the NFL's New York Jets were pushing for a $2.2 billion stadium and convention center on the Far West Side of Manhattan, which would be converted into an Olympic stadium if the city won its bid to host for the 2012 Summer Games.

After the Jets' proposal fell through everything came to a head in July 2005 when the Mets agreed to finance all construction costs with the city paying for all infrastructure improvements. The one extra stipulation was that if the city did win the Olympic bid the Mets would vacate the stadium for all of 2012 (and probably play at new Yankee Stadium) so it could be expanded to host the opening and closing ceremonies and track and field, reminiscent of what occurred in Atlanta for the 1996 Summer Games.

Obviously that part didn't happen.

Congratulations, you will now be quizzed on none of that:

The Stadiums

1. Where did the Mets play their first two seasons?
2. Who was the opponent during the Mets' first home game and what was the result?
3. Who hit the first home run for the Mets in a home game?
4. Who is Shea Stadium named after?
5. What was Shea Stadium originally supposed to be named?
6. What did Shea Stadium initially cost to build?
7. What was used to christen the new stadium?
8. What major sporting venue was across the street?
9. What team was the opponent during the Mets' first home game at Shea Stadium and what was the result?
10. What other sports franchise initially called Shea Stadium home?

11. What band performed the first concert at Shea Stadium on August 15, 1965?
12. Who else called Shea Stadium home in 1975?
13. What famous baseball moment did President Bill Clinton participate in at Shea Stadium on April 15, 1997?
14. Who did the Mets play during the final game at Shea Stadium in 2008?
15. Who was the opponent for the Mets' first home game at Citi Field and what was the result?
16. What "first" occurred with the leadoff batter?
17. Who hit the first inside-the-park home run at Citi Field?
18. Who made the first error in the stadium?
19. Before the Mets came back from spring training, what two college programs played in the first sporting event at Citi Field?
20. How much did Citi Field cost to build?

Answers

1. The Polo Grounds
2. The Pittsburgh Pirates, who won 4–3 on April 13, 1962.
3. Frank Thomas off Tom Sturdivant, who still got the win.
4. William A. Shea, a prominent New York attorney who was considered the driving force in the effort to bring National League baseball back to the city after the Dodgers and Giants left for California in 1957.
5. Flushing Meadows Stadium
6. $25 million
7. Shea poured a mixture of water from the Harlem River (near the old Polo Grounds) and the Gowanus Canal (near the site of Ebbets Field) over the infield during a pre-game ceremony.
8. The USTA Billie Jean King National Tennis Center, where the U.S. Open tennis tournament is played every fall.
9. It was the exact same outcome as the first game at the Polo Grounds, the Pittsburgh Pirates won 4–3.
10. The New York Jets
11. The Beatles. It was the first time that a sports stadium was used for a rock concert.
12. The New York Yankees and the New York Giants while Yankee Stadium was being renovated.
13. Jackie Robinson's No. 42 was retired in all of baseball. The President joined Jackie Robinson's widow Rachel for the ceremony.
14. The Florida Marlins. The Mets lost 4–2.

15. The Mets lost to the San Diego Padres, 6–5.
16. Jody Gerut became the first player in Major League history to open a new ballpark with a leadoff home run.
17. Angel Pagan vs. Philadelphia off Pedro Martinez on August 23, 2009.
18. Ryan Church on a dropped fly ball.
19. St. John's and Georgetown
20. $850 million

Five

Nicknames

What's in a nickname? A lot, especially when it comes to naming a sports organization.

New York has been home to some epic and unique franchises, and not just in baseball with the Yankees, Dodgers, and Giants. The Knickerbockers, Rangers, and Islanders are all distinctive in their own rights just like Cosmos in soccer.

When it came to naming the expansion baseball team, officials decided to reach out to fans and have them choose between 10 suggested finalists: Avengers, Bees, Burros, Continentals, Jets, Mets, NYBS, Rebels, Skyliners and Skyscrapers.

They received 2,563 mailed entries, including 9,613 suggestions and 644 different names. The top vote-getter by a wide margin was Mets, followed by two write-in names, Empires and Islanders.

The *New York Times* noted, "what the fans will call the team when it begins play, of course, will depend in part on how it performs," but added that another appealing aspect to the name was "it has a brevity that will delight headline writers."

According to the Mets' media guide it was considered the one that best met five basic criteria:

It met public and press acceptance;

It was closely related to the team's corporate name;

It was descriptive of the metropolitan area;

It had a brevity that delighted copy readers everywhere;

It had historical background referring to the Metropolitans of the 19th century American Association.

Nicknames

Who, or what, had the following nicknames?

1. King Kong
2. The Italian Stallion
3. The Franchise
4. Grant's Tomb
5. Kid
6. The Old Perfessor
7. Doc
8. Goose Koufax
9. Cooz
10. Fonzie
11. Ho Jo
12. Coney
13. The Bad Guys
14. The Miracle Worker
15. Mex
16. El Sid
17. Monster
18. Thor
19. The Hammer
20. Mags
21. The Real Deal
22. Cabbage Patch
23. Nails
24. Bad Dude
25. Captain America

Answers

1. Dave Kingman, although some called him Big Bird.
2. Lee Mazzilli
3. Tom Seaver, who was also called Tom Terrific.
4. Shea Stadium due to the falling attendance after general manager M. Donald Grant traded away Tom Seaver.
5. Gary Carter
6. Casey Stengel
7. Dwight Gooden

 8. Tom Gorman
 9. Jerry Koosman
10. Edgardo Alfonzo
11. Howard Johnson
12. David Cone
13. The 1986 Mets
14. Gil Hodges
15. Keith Hernandez (even though he wasn't Mexican)
16. Sid Fernandez
17. Mike Piazza (who was also called Pizza Man)
18. Noah Syndergaard
19. John Milner
20. Dave Magadan
21. Matt Harvey (who is also called "the Dark Knight")
22. Wally Backman
23. Lenny Dykstra (who was also called "The Dude")
24. John Stearns
25. David Wright

Noah Syndergaard has a divine nickname. (Jon Barash)

Six

The Greats

Tom Seaver

To many fans there's really just one New York Met who clearly stands out among all the rest, Tom Seaver.

The three-time Cy Young Award winner became the face of the franchise and one of the most dominant pitchers in Major League Baseball history.

He joined the team when it was horrible, a perennial cellar-dweller in the standings, and helped turn it into a World Series champion. Seaver was the National League Rookie of the Year in 1967, named to 12 All-Star teams, led the National League in wins and ERA three times, and in strikeouts five times.

Teammate Cleon Jones once said, "Tom does everything well. He's the kind of man you'd want your kids to grow up to be like. Tom's a studious player, devoted to his profession, a loyal cat, trustworthy—everything a Boy Scout's supposed to be. In fact, we call him 'Boy Scout.'"

In an ESPN poll, Hall of Famers Bob Gibson, Juan Marichal, Jim Palmer, Nolan Ryan, Steve Carlton, Bert Blyleven, and Don Sutton all said Tom Seaver was the best pitcher of their generation.

He ranks first in franchise wins (198), ERA (2.57), strikeouts (2,541) and games started (395), and those in second place aren't very close.

Tom Seaver talks to reporters in the locker room after throwing a one-hit shutout against the Chicago Cubs on July 9, 1969.

When Seaver was elected to the National Baseball Hall of Fame in 1992 he received a record 98.84 percent of the vote. He was left off five ballots and Hall of Fame vice president for communications and education Jeff Idelson told *USA Today* in 2006 that technically Seaver should have missed perfection by just one vote.

"Three voters submitted blank ballots in protest of Pete Rose [for not being on the ballot]," Idelson said. "Another, following open-heart surgery, overlooked Seaver after filling out his ballot, and a fifth said he didn't vote for first-time eligibles. Seaver should have missed by one, assuming four of the five would have voted for him."

Seaver wasn't the first one to be inducted into the Mets Hall of Fame, or the first to have his jersey number retired by the franchise, but he gets listed here first:

 # Tom Seaver

1. Where was Tom Seaver born on November 17, 1944?
2. What "team" did he join on June 28, 1962?
3. For which major college did he pitch?
4. Before getting a scholarship, which summer-league team did he play for in order to show his worthiness?
5. Which team drafted Seaver in the 10th round after his sophomore year?
6. Why was his contract with the Atlanta Braves in 1966 voided by Commissioner William Eckert?
7. How did the Mets acquire the signing rights to Seaver?
8. What Hall of Fame player called Tom Seaver "The toughest pitcher I've ever faced"?
9. What minor-league team did Seaver play for in 1966?
10. How many games did Tom Seaver win during both of his first two seasons with the Mets?
11. What statistical accomplishment did Seaver do only once during his career, but he also matched in the 1967 All-Star Game?
12. Starting in 1968, how many consecutive seasons did Seaver strike out at least 200 batters?
13. In 1969 who beat out Seaver for the Most Valuable Player Award in the National League?
14. On July 9, 1969, who broke up Seaver's bid for a perfect game with one out in the ninth inning at Shea Stadium?
15. In addition to tying Steve Carlton's Major League record with 19 strikeouts in a nine-inning game, what record did Seaver set during the 2–1 victory over the San Diego Padres at Shea Stadium on April 22, 1970?

16. Although many consider 1971 to be Seaver's finest season, with a 20–10 record, 1.76 ERA, and 289 strikeouts, who was named the National League's Cy Young Award winner?

17. Who said of Seaver: "Blind men come to the park just to hear him pitch?"

18. Who said: "My idea of managing is giving the ball to Tom Seaver and sitting down and watching him work."

19. How many one-hitters did Seaver throw for the Mets?

20. What unusual statistical accomplishment did Seaver pull off against the Milwaukee Brewers on May 9, 1984?

21. In what city did Seaver record his 300th career victory?

22. Who was being honored by the home team that day?

23. With which Major League team did Seaver end his career?

24. Against which team did he earn the final win of his career, No. 311?

25. What record did Seaver set when he was elected into the Baseball Hall of Fame on January 7, 1992?

Answers

1. Fresno, California.
2. He joined the United States Marine Corps Reserves.
3. Southern California
4. The Alaska Goldpanners of Fairbanks, Alaska
5. The Los Angeles Dodgers
6. Because his college team had played in two exhibition games. The NCAA then ruled Seaver ineligible because he had signed a pro contract (but intended to play the college season).
7. After Seaver's father threatened a lawsuit MLB teams were allowed to match the Braves' initial offer and sign Seaver. The Mets were one of three teams that did and won a drawing with the Philadelphia Phillies and Cleveland Indians for his rights.
8. Hank Aaron
9. Jacksonville Suns of the International League
10. 16
11. He had one official save during the 1968 season, and got the save in the 1967 All-Star Game by pitching a scoreless 15th inning.
12. Nine
13. Willie McCovey
14. Chicago Cubs rookie backup outfielder Jimmy Qualls with a single to left field.
15. He struck out the final 10 batters in a game.
16. Ferguson Jenkins of the Chicago Cubs.
17. Reggie Jackson
18. Sparky Anderson, who managed Seaver with the Cincinnati Reds in 1977–78.
19. Five
20. He won two games. Seaver pitched the final inning of a game suspended the day before, getting the win in relief, and then started and won the game scheduled.
21. New York, but it was at Yankee Stadium.
22. It was Phil Rizzuto Day. Rizzuto and Seaver would later form a broadcast team for the Yankees.
23. The Boston Red Sox
24. The Minnesota Twins, on August 18, 1986
25. He received the highest-ever percentage of votes. Ken Griffey Jr. broke it in 2016.

Casey Stengel

1. When and where was Casey Stengel born?
2. Why was he called Casey?
3. As a player, what position did he play?
4. How many teams did he play for in the major leagues? Name them.
5. Why did Dodgers' owner Charles Ebbets trade Stengel to the Pittsburgh Pirates?
6. As a player, how many World Series did Stengel participate in?
7. Although he never played for the Yankees what was his claim to fame at old Yankee Stadium?
8. Which college did Stengel serve as an assistant coach for in 1914?
9. What was Stengel's first job as a minor-league manager?
10. With what team did he win his first championship as a manager?
11. With what team was Stengel hired as the manager over the objections of its owner?
12. In 1950, when Phil Rizzuto got a letter threatening his life along with three of his teammates, with whom did Stengel have him switch jerseys?
13. In 1953 what did Stengel become the first, and only, manager to do?
14. What team did the Mets have to hire him away from?
15. What got Stengel to retire for good on August 30, 1965?
16. Which team was the first to retire his jersey, the Mets or the Yankees?
17. When Stengel would say, "You can look it up," to what accomplishment was he referring?
18. How and when was Stengel selected for the Hall of Fame?
19. In three-and-a-half years, how many games did Stengel lose with the Mets?
20. Where did Stengel die on September 29, 1975?

Answers

1. July 30, 1890, in Kansas City, Missouri
2. Because he was from K.C.—Kansas City.
3. Outfielder, mostly in right field.
4. Five: Dodgers/Robins, Pirates, Phillies, Giants and Braves
5. Stengel kept holding out at the start of the season in contract disputes.
6. Three, in 1916 for the Dodgers and in 1922 and 1923 for the Giants.
7. Stengel hit the first home run in the stadium.
8. Ole Miss
9. The Worcester Panthers of the Eastern League.
10. The Toledo Mud Hens of the American Association
11. The minor-league Milwaukee Brewers in 1944. Owner Bill Veeck was serving in the South Pacific in the Marines during World War II. Stengel led the Brewers to the American Association pennant.
12. Billy Martin
13. Manage a team to five consecutive World Series titles (1949–1953).
14. None. He had "involuntarily" retired from the Yankees at age 70.
15. He broke his hip after falling off a bar stool.
16. The Mets did it in 1965. The Yankees waited until 1970.
17. Stengel is the only man to have worn the uniform, as player or manager, of all four Major League teams in New York City in the 20th century: the New York Giants (player), the Brooklyn Dodgers (both a player and a manager), the New York Yankees (manager), and the New York Mets (manager).
18. Veteran's Committee in 1966.
19. .404
20. Glendale, California

Gil Hodges

1. Where was Gil Hodges born?
2. What college did Hodges attend in hopes of someday becoming a collegiate coach?
3. Which Major League organization did he turn down an offer from in 1941 in order to go to school?
4. In which branch of the U.S. Armed Forces did Hodges serve during World War II?
5. What position did Hodges initially play for the Brooklyn Dodgers and why did he switch to first base?
6. How many All-Star Games did he play in?
7. How many World Series titles did he win as a player?
8. How many Gold Gloves did he win?
9. When Hodges retired with 370 home runs, who was the only right-handed hitter in Major League history with more?
10. On August 31, 1950, against the Boston Braves, Hodges became just the second player since 1900 to do what?
11. What "claim to fame" could Hodges claim from the 1952 World Series against the Yankees?
12. What National League record did he hold for 17 years, from 1957–74?
13. How did Hodges officially join the Mets?
14. Who did they re-acquire for him from the Washington Senators in 1963?
15. In 1965, what Senators pitcher did Hodges talk out of committing suicide?
16. During his first season managing the Mets how many games did they win?
17. What memorable move did Hodges make during the second game of a July 30 doubleheader against the Houston Astros?
18. What was he awarded from New York City in 1969?
19. Although he was never named the league MVP, how many years did he receive votes in the balloting?
20. How old was Hodges when he died on April 2, 1972?

Answers

1. Princeton, Indiana
2. St. Joseph's College
3. The Detroit Tigers
4. The Marine Corps. He was an anti-aircraft gunner in the battles of Tinian and Okinawa, and received a Bronze Star Medal with Combat "V" for heroism under fire.
5. Hodges was originally a catcher, but switched to first base due to the development of Roy Campanella.
6. Eight (1949–1955, 1957)
7. Three (1955, 1959, 1969)
8. Three (1957–79)
9. Jimmie Foxx. Hodges was 10th overall.
10. He hit four home runs in a game that didn't go to extra innings. Lou Gehrig was the first player to do so.
11. He went hitless in all seven games, going 0-for-21.
12. Career grand slams
13. He was selected in the expansion draft.
14. Outfielder Jimmy Piersall
15. Pitcher Ryne Duren
16. .73, at that point a team record.
17. When Mets left fielder Cleon Jones failed to hustle after a ball hit to the outfield Hodges slowly walked out to left field to remove Jones and then walked him back to the dugout.
18. The Bronze Medallion, New York City's highest civilian honor.
19. Nine
20. .47

Bud Harrelson

1. What's Bud Harrelson's real full name?
2. On what famous day was he born?
3. Where did he attend college?
4. When Harrelson played his first game in the majors at the age of 21, how much did he weigh?
5. What's Harrelson's biggest claim to fame within the Mets organization?
6. What's he best known for outside of that?
7. What major honor did he receive for the first time during the 1970 season?
8. What National League record did Harrelson set in 1970? (Bonus: Who holds the record as of 2015?)
9. What major honor did he receive after the 1971 season?
10. Although he received consideration, what killed his chances of being named the National League's Most Valuable Player in 1971?
11. How many times did he draw a walk that season?
12. What were the most home runs Harrelson hit in a single season?
13. True or false, Harrelson had a better career postseason than regular-season batting average?
14. Who did Harrelson replace on the 1985 Mets coaching staff?
15. Who did he replace as manager in 1990?
16. True or false, Harrelson had a winning record during his two-year stint as the Mets' manager?
17. Who replaced him near the end of the 1991 season?
18. What two other teams did Harrelson play for after leaving the Mets?
19. Which famous rival of his was a teammate on one of those teams?
20. On what TV show did he make a cameo appearance in 1999?

Answers

1. Derrel McKinley Harrelson
2. D-Day, June 6, 1944, in Niles, California.
3. San Francisco State
4. 147 pounds
5. He's the only person to be in a Mets uniform for the club's two World Series Championships, as a player in 1969 and a coach in 1986.
6. Getting into a fight with Pete Rose during the 1973 National League Championship Series.
7. Harrelson was named to the National League's All-Star Team.
8. He set the record for consecutive errorless games played at shortstop during a season with 54. Rey Ordonez had 100 consecutive errorless games in 1999 (10 shy of the Major League record set by Mike Bordick in 2002).
9. He won a Gold Glove Award.
10. Harrelson's .243 batting average
11. 95
12. One. He did it seven times.
13. False. He hit .236 in the regular season, .200 in the postseason.
14. Bobby Valentine, who was hired to be the manager of the Texas Rangers.
15. Davey Johnson
16. True. His teams were 145–129.
17. Mike Cubbage
18. The Phillies (1978–79) and Texas Rangers (1980)
19. Pete Rose
20. *Everybody Loves Raymond*

Rusty Staub

1. On what day was Rusty Staub born in New Orleans?
2. Who nicknamed Daniel Joseph Staub "Rusty?"
3. Staub is the only player in Major League history to have at least 500 hits with four different teams. Name them.
4. How many times was he named to play in an All-Star Game?
5. How did Staub end up on the expansion Montreal Expos?
6. Why was the deal amended?
7. A fan favorite in Montreal after learning to speak French, what did they affectionately they call Staub?
8. Who was the pitcher when Staub got the first base hit in Montreal Expos history?
9. During his first season with the Mets, who hit Staub with a pitch in the wrist, resulting in a fracture that he played with until an X-Ray revealed the broken bone?
10. Despite having a shoulder injury that forced him to throw underhand, what did Staub hit during the 1973 World Series?
11. When Staub was injury free in 1974, in which statistical category did he lead the Mets: hits, runs batted in, or at-bats?
12. Who all was involved in the trade that sent Staub to the Detroit Tigers before the 1976 season?
13. What unusual role did Staub serve with the Mets in 1982?
14. What did he lead the National League in in both 1983 and 1984?
15. What Major League record set by Dave Philley in 1958 did he tie?
16. What Major League record did he tie that was shared by Joe Cronin in 1943, and Jerry Lynch in 1961?
17. Which franchise retired his jersey number?
18. Staub hit a home run in all 23 seasons he was on a Major Leaguer roster. Who are the only two players with longer such streaks?

19. Staub is one of four players to hit a home run in the major leagues both as a teenager and over the age of 40. Who are the other three?

20. After his playing career ended, what charitable organization did Staub found?

Answers

1. April Fools Day, April 1, 1944
2. According to Baseball: The Biographical Encyclopedia, by Matthew Silverman, right after he was born one of the nurses nicknamed him Rusty due to the red fuzz he had all over his head.
3. The Houston Colt .45s/Astros, the Montreal Expos, the New York Mets, and the Detroit Tigers
4. Six (1967–1971, 1976)
5. Staub was traded to the Expos for Don Clendenon and Jesús Alou.
6. Don Clendenon refused to report to the Astros and attempted to retire. After the commissioner's office got involved Clendenon stayed with the Expos, but the Astros instead received Jack Billingham, Skip Guinn, and $100,000 as compensation.
7. "Le Grand Orange"
8. Tom Seaver
9. Future teammate George Stone of the Atlanta Braves. The injury never quite healed right.
10. .423 with a home run and six RBIs
11. Actually, all three
12. Staub was traded along with pitcher Mickey Lolich and outfielder Billy Baldwin.
13. Player-coach
14. Pinch-hits and pinch-hit RBIs
15. Most consecutive pinch hits in a season, eight
16. Staub drove in 25 runs while pinch hitting.
17. The Expos, No. 10
18. Rickey Henderson (25 seasons) and Ty Cobb (24 seasons)
19. Ty Cobb, Gary Sheffield and Alex Rodriguez
20. In 1986 he founded the New York Police and Children's Benefit Fund. During its first 15 years of existence it raised and distributed $11 million for families of policemen and firefighters killed in the line of duty. After the terrorist attacks of September 11, 2001, it received contributions in excess of $112 million.

Jerry Koosman

1. Where was Jerry Koosman born on December 23, 1942?
2. What high school did he attend?
3. Who was said to have discovered Koosman?
4. The Mets nearly released Koosman in 1966? Why didn't they?
5. In 1967 what statistical category did Koosman lead the International League in?
6. How old was Koosman when he made his Major League debut?
7. During his first year in the Mets rotation how many games did he win?
8. Who did Koosman strike out to end a scoreless ninth inning and earn a save in the 1968 All-Star Game?
9. Who did Koosman finish second to in 1968 Rookie of the Year voting?
10. In August/September how many consecutive scoreless innings did Koosman throw to set a Mets record?
11. In what year did Koosman have a career best 21 wins and 200 strikeouts?
12. Who did he lose out to for the Cy Young award that year?
13. After Tom Seaver was traded how many games did Koosman lose in 1977?
14. After going 3–15 in 1978 who did the Mets trade Koosman to and what pitcher did they get in return?
15. How many wins did he post during the subsequent season with that team?
16. With Koosman's departure, who was the last remaining member of the 1969 Miracle Mets?
17. With which team did Koosman make his final postseason appearance?
18. With 222 career wins which Detroit Tigers pitcher is he tied with on the all-time list?
19. With which team did Koosman go 0–20 for during the 1984–85 seasons?
20. Who are the only two pitchers to post more wins for the Mets than Koosman's 140?

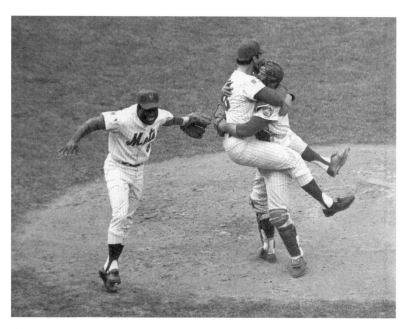

Catcher Jerry Grote embraces Jerry Koosman as Ed Charles skips past after the Mets closed out Game 5 against the Orioles to clinch the 1969 title.

Answers

1. Appleton, Minnesota
2. West Central School of Agriculture High School in Morris, Minnesota
3. The son of a Shea Stadium usher who saw Koosman pitch while in the Army at Fort Bliss, Texas. He wrote to his father about Koosman and the Mets eventually offered a contract after his discharge from the military.
4. He owed the franchise money, which had been wired to him after his car broke down en route to spring training.
5. Strikeouts, with 183
6. 24
7. 19, to go with seven shutouts and a 2.08 ERA. All three were franchise records.
8. Carl Yastrzemski. The final score was 1–0.
9. Johnny Bench
10. 31⅔ consecutive scoreless innings.
11. 1976
12. Randy Jones

13. 20. He tied Phil Niekro for most losses in the National League.
14. The Minnesota Twins for a player to be named later, who ended up being Jesse Orosco.
15. 20
16. Ed Kranepool
17. The Chicago White Sox in 1983. He was 40 years old.
18. Hooks Dauss
19. Philadelphia Phillies
20. Tom Seaver (198) and Dwight Gooden (157).

Ed Kranepool, just 17 years old when he signed with the Mets, stands with his mother, Ethel Kranepool, as they visit the Polo Grounds. (John Lindsay)

Ed Kranepool

1. Where was Kranepool born on November 8, 1944?
2. Where did he go to school?
3. How old was Kranepool when he made his Major League debut?
4. What number did he initially wear?
5. What did he switch to and why?
6. What season was Kranepool named to the All-Star Game?
7. What did he end up hitting that season, and why was that such an ominous sign for the Mets?
8. Who did Kranepool hit two home runs against to help spark the initial 11-game winning streak by the Miracle Mets in 1969?
9. What was Kranepool's only hit in the 1969 World Series?
10. What happened during the 1970 season that nearly caused Kranepool to retire from baseball?
11. Whose funeral in 1975 did Kranepool believe he was the only Mets player to be invited to?
12. Who was handed a note during the 1973 playoffs that read: "Kranepool flies to right. Agnew resigns."?
13. In what statistical category did he lead the National League in 1971?
14. In 1971, Kranepool had a career high in home runs. How many did he hit?
15. Who was traded in 1978, making Kranepool the last of the Miracle Mets?
16. Who once said of Kranepool: "He's only seventeen and he runs like he's thirty."?
17. Which number was greater, his number of stolen bases or times caught stealing?
18. How old was Kranepool when he retired?
19. Which other teams did Kranepool play for?
20. When Kranepool finished his career he was the team leader in hits and doubles. How many did he have?

Answers

1. New York, which would later help make him a huge hometown favorite.
2. James Monroe High School in the Bronx
3. Kranepool was 17 years old when he broke into the big leagues on September 22, 1962. He was six years younger than the next-youngest teammate.
4. 21
5. The Mets acquired pitcher Warren Spahn from the Milwaukee Braves, who had worn No. 21. So he began wearing number 7.
6. 1965
7. He led the team in hitting with 133 hits and 24 doubles.
8. The Los Angeles Dodgers
9. A home run in Game 3. He finished the Series 1-for-4.
10. He was demoted to the minors on June 23 after batting just .118.
11. Owner Joan Payson
12. Supreme Court Justice Potter Stewart, who was a big baseball fan.
13. Fielding percentage (.998)
14. .14
15. Jerry Koosman
16. Manager Casey Stengel
17. Kranepool had 15 stolen bases and was caught stealing 27 times during his career.
18. .34
19. None. His entire 18-year career was with the Mets.
20. 1,418 hits and 225 doubles. He played in 1,853 games and had 5,436 plate appearances.

Cleon Jones

1. Where was Cleon Jones born?
2. At what college was he a standout baseball and football player?
3. How was he acquired by the Mets organization?
4. When Jones was first called up to the majors in which minor leagues had he played?
5. During his second September call-up in 1965 what was his batting average?
6. Against which team did he hit his first Major League home run?
7. In 1966 what place did Jones finish in National League Rookie of the Year voting?
8. Why did Jones go from primarily playing center field to left field in 1968?
9. During which season did Jones start in the All-Star Game?
10. What did he do at the plate in the All-Star Game?
11. What unusual occurrence involving Jones occurred during the July 30, 1969, doubleheader against the Houston Astros, which some believe sparked the Miracle Mets' late-season rally?
12. Who were the only two players in the National League to have a better batting average than Jones in 1969?
13. Despite hitting .429 in the National League Championship Series, what was Jones best known for during the 1969 playoffs?
14. How long of a hitting streak did Jones have in 1970, which was then a team record?
15. Against which opponent did Jones have his first career two–home run game in the 1973 season opener?
16. What was the "Ball on the Wall" play?
17. With which team did Jones play his final Major League game?
18. How many career outfield assists did he have?

19. What's the name of the rap group and the song in which Jones is mentioned?

20. In what movie is Jones referred to?

Answers

1. Plateau, Alabama, on August 4, 1942

2. Alabama A&M

3. Jones signed as an amateur free agent.

4. Jones had played for the Carolina League's Raleigh Mets, and the New York-Penn League Auburn Mets, when he received a September call-up to the major league club in 1963 without having played double- or triple-A ball.

5. .149 in 74 at-bats

6. The Pittsburgh Pirates

7. Fourth. He hit .275 with eight home runs, 57 RBIs and 16 stolen bases.

8. The Mets acquired Jones' childhood friend Tommie Agee from the Chicago White Sox, and he took over in center field.

9. 1969. Jones batted .341 with 10 home runs and 56 RBIs during the first half of the season.

10. He went 2-for-4 with two runs scored as the National League won 9—3.

11. In the middle of an inning manager Gil Hodges left the dugout and talked to Jones in left field before pulling him. Neither the player nor the manager ever publicly revealed what was said between them on the field.

12. Pete Rose and Roberto Clemente. Jones batted .340.

13. Catching the fly ball for the final out of the World Series.

14. 23 games

15. The Philadelphia Phillies. He had his second later during that season against the Pittsburgh Pirates

16. During a crucial three-game September series against the Pittsburgh Pirates, Dave Augustine hit what appeared to be a two-run home run over the left-field wall in the 13ᵗʰ inning. Hoping it would stay in play he turned to make a play off the wall when the ball hit the top of the wall and went right into Jones' glove on the fly. He fired to relay man Wayne Garrett, who threw home to catcher Ron Hodges to nail Richie Zisk trying to score from first.

17. The Chicago White Sox

18. 64—83 overall as he also played first base some.

19. *B-Boy Document '99* by the group High and Mighty.

20. *Men in Black 3*. It features a scene in which the Mets win the 1969 World Series.

Jerry Grote

1. Where was Gerald Wayne Grote born on October 6, 1942?
2. What major event occurred when he was 10 years old?
3. Where did he attend college?
4. Fittingly, with which team did he make his Major League debut on September 21, 1963?
5. Although Grote only played three games that season, what was he a part of on September 27th with the expansion team?
6. What unusual situation was he behind the plate for on April 23, 1964?
7. Who did the Mets give up to acquire Grote in a trade?
8. Grote was so competitive what was he known for doing after his pitcher ended an inning with a strikeout?
9. With Grote the everyday catcher and anchoring the pitching staffs in 1966, what did the Mets avoid for the first time in franchise history?
10. What prestigious honor did Grote receive during the 1968 season?
11. With Grote calling the pitches, what did the Orioles hit during the 1969 World Series?
12. What Major League record did Grote set on April 22, 1970?
13. Why did Grote miss two months of the 1973 season?
14. During what year was Grote named to his second All-Star Game?
15. What happened the first time Grote faced former teammate Tug McGraw in 1975?
16. What happened the only time Grote batted against Seaver?
17. Which team lured Grote out of retirement in 1981?
18. With which team did he play his final Major League game?
19. How many Gold Gloves did Grote win during his 16-year career?
20. Who once said "If Grote and I were on the same team, I would be playing third base."?

Answers

1. San Antonio, Texas
2. His family was caught in an F-4 tornado. His mother, father, and two sisters all made it to safety, but his grandmother was killed.
3. Trinity College
4. The Houston Colt .45s
5. Every starter in the lineup was a rookie.
6. Ken Johnson became the first pitcher in major league history to lose a complete-game no-hitter in nine innings.
7. Tom Parsons
8. He would roll the ball to the far side of the pitcher's mound (closest to the Mets' dugout) so the opposing team's pitcher had to walk further to retrieve the ball.
9. 100 losses and last place
10. He started in the All-Star Game. Although known as a defensive catcher he was batting over .300 at midseason.
11. .146
12. Grote set a major league record with 20 putouts in a game when Tom Seaver struck out 19 San Diego Padres.
13. He broke a bone in his right arm when hit by a pitch. The team's rise in the standings occurred after he returned.
14. 1974
15. With the Mets down 3–2 he hit a game-winning two-run home run.
16. He struck out.
17. The Kansas City Royals. His seven RBIs on June 3, 1981, set a franchise record that has been tied numerous times since then.
18. The Los Angeles Dodgers
19. None
20. Johnny Bench, who was the perennial Gold Glove winner at catcher.

Tug McGraw

1. What's Tug McGraw's real name?
2. What was his father's nickname?
3. What's the origin of the "Tug" nickname?
4. Where was McGraw born on August 30, 1944?
5. Where did he go to school after high school?
6. How many innings did McGraw pitch while earning his first Major League win?
7. Who did he beat to earn his second win, and what milestone was it for the franchise?
8. Where did McGraw report on September 23, 1965?
9. Who went with him?
10. Where did he later train?
11. Which franchise lost its first-ever game to the Mets with McGraw the winning pitcher?
12. As part of the Miracle Mets how many games did McGraw appear in in the 1969 World Series?
13. What unusual accomplishment for a relief pitcher did McGraw do on September 8, 1971?
14. What did McGraw do during his first All-Star Game appearance in 1972?
15. How many saves did he finish with that season?
16. How many appearances did he make during the 1973 World Series?
17. Name everyone who was included in the trade to send McGraw to the Philadelphia Phillies on December 3, 1974.
18. Who did McGraw strike out to record the final out of the 1980 World Series?
19. McGraw was the last active major leaguer to have played under which manager?
20. Who is McGraw's son?

Answers

1. Frank Edwin McGraw, Jr
2. Big Mac
3. He aggressively breast-fed.
4. Martinez, California
5. Solano Community College
6. Nine. He broke into the majors as a starter and threw a complete-game win against the St Louis Cardinals on August 22, 1965.
7. Sandy Koufax. It was the first time the Mets beat the Los Angeles Dodgers legend.
8. To the Marine Corps Recruit Depot Parris Island to be trained as a rifleman.
9. Mets pitcher Jim Bethke
10. Marine Corps Base Camp Lejeune
11. The Montreal Expos on April 9, 1969
12. None. His only postseason appearance was in Game 2 of the National League Championship Series.
13. He hit his only career home run against the Montreal Expos.
14. McGraw pitched two innings, striking out four and giving up only one hit to earn the win in the National League's 4–3 come-from-behind victory.
15. 27, setting a Mets record that stood until 1984.
16. Five
17. McGraw was traded along with outfielders Don Hahn and Dave Schneck to the Philadelphia Phillies for pitcher Mac Scarce, outfielder Del Unser, and catcher John Stearns.
18. Kansas City Royals left fielder Willie Wilson
19. Casey Stengel
20. Country singer Tim McGraw

Manager Gil Hodges hits to pitcher Tug McGraw during Spring Training in St. Petersburg, Florida, before the 1971 season.

Mookie Wilson

1. True or false, "Mookie" was his given name.
2. Where was he born?
3. How many brothers and sisters did he have?
4. What three colleges was he associated with?
5. Which team initially drafted him in 1976?
6. What major honor did he win in the minor leagues?
7. How old was Wilson when he broke into the majors?
8. Who did manager Joe Torre move from center field to left field to make room for Wilson in the lineup?
9. In 1982, what associate of Wilson did the Mets draft?
10. Whose team record for stolen bases did Wilson break in 1982?
11. Who did he surpass to become the Mets' all-time stolen base king in 1984?
12. During spring training in 1986 who accidentally hit Wilson in the eye with a throw during base-running drills?
13. On the famous ground ball that went through Bill Buckner's legs during Game 6 of the World Series, in what slot of the batting order was Wilson batting?
14. What was the count on the pitch he hit?
15. Who did the Mets acquire prior to the start of the 1987 season, which made for a crowded outfield and players sharing time?
16. What was Wilson's reaction?
17. Two years later who did the Mets acquire in a trade for Wilson on July 31, 1989?
18. On the same day who did the Toronto Blue Jays also acquire via waivers?
19. What did Wilson do during the three-game series on his first trip back to Fenway Park since 1986?
20. After his career was over, what major baseball award was Mookie Wilson presented in 2006?

Answers

1. False. It's William Hayward Wilson.
2. Bamberg, South Carolina
3. 11
4. He signed with South Carolina State, but days later the baseball program was discontinued. So instead he attended Spartanburg Methodist College and then transferred to South Carolina.
5. The Los Angeles Dodgers in the fourth round. He didn't sign and gambled that he would be a better draft pick in 1977. He was—the Mets took him in the second round.
6. Wilson was named the International League's Rookie of the Year in 1979.
7. 24
8. Lee Mazzilli
9. His brother John in the 17th round.
10. Frank Tavares
11. Lee Mazzilli
12. Mets shortstop Rafael Santana. Wilson needed 21 stitches.
13. Seventh
14. Full, 3–2
15. Kevin McReynolds
16. He asked for a trade. The Mets didn't give him one.
17. Reliever Jeff Musselman and minor league pitcher Mike Brady from the Toronto Blue Jays
18. Lee Mazzilli
19. He went 9-for-14 (.643) with four runs scored and an RBI as the Blue Jays swept the series.
20. The Willie, Mickey, and the Duke Award from the New York Baseball Writers Association

Keith Hernandez

1. Where was Keith Hernandez born on October 20, 1953?
2. Which future major leaguer did he go to high school with?
3. In what round was he selected in the 1971 draft?
4. Because of his development, who did the St. Louis Cardinals trade away to make room for Hernandez at first base?
5. What number did Hernandez wear during his first two seasons, what did he switch to and who did he want to honor with this jersey number?
6. Who did he share the 1979 National League MVP award with?
7. Who did Hernandez get a game-tying two-RBI single off of in Game 7 of the 1982 World Series, on his 29th birthday?
8. With whom did Hernandez regularly butt heads, leading to his trade to the Mets?
9. Why did Hernandez switch to No. 17?
10. Who did Hernandez finish second to in 1984 MVP voting?
11. What rare accomplishment did Hernandez do during a 19-inning game against the Atlanta Braves on July 14, 1985?
12. What did Hernandez do defensively that's now illegal?
13. What did Pete Rose once compare to "driving the lane against Bill Russell"?
14. In what category that's no longer considered an official statistic did Hernandez set a record in 1985?
15. When the Mets rallied with two outs in the 10th inning of Game 6 of the 1986 World Series, where was Hernandez?
16. How many consecutive Gold Gloves did Hernandez win?
17. Which team did Hernandez play for during his final season?
18. Which pitcher wore No. 17 with the Mets in honor of Hernandez?
19. Which Mets pitchers wore No. 17 when they played for other teams?

20. What was Hernandez's base salary when he entered the major leagues, and what was his biggest salary?

21. On September 27, 2012, what did Hernandez famously do for charity?

Answers

1. San Francisco
2. Bob McClure
3. 42nd. He was the 776th player selected.
4. Joe Torre to the Mets for Tommy Moore and Ray Sadecki.
5. He wore No. 18, but switched to 37. He wanted a number with 7 in it to honor Mickey Mantle.
6. Willie Stargell. It's the only time the award has been shared.
7. Bob McClure
8. Manager Whitey Herzog
9. Because the Mets had already retired No. 37.
10. Ryne Sandberg
11. Hit for the cycle. His plate appearances, in order: 2B, LO, 3B, FO, HR, FO, 1B, BB, GO, FO, GO
12. He would position himself essentially in foul territory along the line so he could make a quicker tag on a base runner.
13. Trying to bunt on Hernandez.
14. Game-winning RBIs with 24. It was only an official statistic from 1980–88, but Hernandez finished with the career mark of 129.
15. After making the second out, Hernandez headed to Davey Johnson's office and opened a beer.
16. 11
17. The Cleveland Indians
18. David Cone
19. Ron Darling, Bob Ojeda, and Roger McDowell
20. He made $15,000 in 1974 and $2 million in 1989.
21. He had his mustache shaved off.

Gary Carter

1. In what state was Gary Carter born on April 8, 1954?
2. What national competition did he win at age 7?
3. With which college football program did he sign a letter of intent to play quarterback?
4. At what position was he drafted?
5. What did Carter do to help himself in Montreal after being drafted by the Expos?
6. Against which team did he make his Major League debut during the second game of a doubleheader on September 16, 1974?
7. Who did he hit his first career home run off of on September 28?
8. Which pitcher did he hit the most home runs off of, with 11?
9. What position did Carter play in his first All-Star Game and what big-name player did he replace?
10. After the 1984 season who did the Expos acquire for Carter from the New York Mets?
11. Against which team did Carter hit a 10th-inning home run for a 6–5 Opening Day victory during his Mets debut?
12. On July 30, 1985, who threw a pitch over Carter's head?
13. What is Carter the only player to do in an All-Star Game and a World Series game?
14. Where did Carter hit career home run No. 300 in 1988?
15. How many career home runs did he hit as a catcher?
16. When Carter broke the Major League record for career putouts by a catcher in 1988, whose record did he break?
17. With which team did he end his playing career?
18. What prestigious award did Carter win in 1989?

Gary Carter congratulates Dwight Gooden after a 7–1 win over the Padres in the first game of a double-header on Sunday, September 7, 1986. (Ray Stubblebine)

19. How many times was he on the Hall of Fame ballot before finally landing enough votes for induction?

20. Where is Gary Carter Stadium located?

Answers

1. California
2. His age division in the NFL's first Punt, Pass & Kick skills competition in 1961.
3. UCLA
4. Shortstop
5. Learn French, making him an instant fan favorite.
6. The New York Mets
7. Steve Carlton
8. Steve Carlton
9. He was a defensive replacement in left field for Pete Rose. Carter spent his first full season in the majors primarily as Montreal's right fielder.
10. Hubie Brooks, Mike Fitzgerald, Herm Winningham, and Floyd Youmans
11. The St. Louis Cardinals
12. Bill Gullickson of his former team, the Montreal Expos
13. Hit two home runs
14. Wrigley Field
15. .298
16. Bill Freehan with 9,941
17. The Montreal Expos
18. The Roberto Clemente Award for his contributions off the field.
19. Six. Carter had joked that he wanted his Cooperstown cap to be a half-and-halfer, split between the Expos and Mets. He went in as an Expo.
20. It's the baseball field at Ahuntsic Park in Montreal

Tommie Agee

1. Where was Tommie Agee born on August 9, 1942?
2. Which college did he attend for a year?
3. With which organization did he sign as a free agent?
4. With which name pitcher was Agee traded to the Chicago White Sox as part of a three-team deal?
5. Who did his former team get in return?
6. After winning the starting job in center field, what did Agee do in the 1966 season opener?
7. What midseason and two major postseason honors did Agee receive?
8. Although Agee struggled at the plate during the second half of the 1967 season and batted just .234, how many of his Chicago White Sox teammates finished with more hits?
9. Who else did the Mets get in the trade with the White Sox for Agee?
10. What happened on the first pitch Agee saw with the Mets during spring training?
11. How bad of a slump did Agee go through during his first season with the Mets in 1968?
12. What two career firsts did Agee experience early in the 1969 season?
13. Why did Agee have a special marker at Shea Stadium?
14. Which media outlet named Agee its 1969 National League Comeback Player of the Year?
15. Which media outlet called his Game 3 the greatest single performance by a center fielder in World Series history?
16. In 1970 Agee set Mets season records for hits, runs, and stolen bases. Give how many he had in one of those categories.
17. What did Agee become the first black player to do in both the American and National leagues?

18. With Agee's career in decline which team did the Mets trade him to following the 1972 season?
19. With which team did Agee play his final Major League game?
20. Which team did Agee spend spring training with in 1974, and was depicted as playing for on his last baseball card, but never did?

Answers

1. Magnolia, Alabama
2. Grambling
3. The Cleveland Indians
4. Tommy John
5. All-Star Rocky Colavito
6. He hit a home run.
7. He represented the White Sox in the All-Star Game and won both the American League Rookie of the Year and Gold Glove awards.
8. Just Don Buford with 129 and hit .241.
9. Al Weis. The Mets gave up Tommy Davis, pitcher Jack Fisher, and two minor leaguers for the offensively-starved White Sox.
10. He was beaned by Bob Gibson.
11. 0-for-34 that brought his batting average down to .102.
12. He had his first multi-home run game (April 10) and first four-hit game (May 2).
13. His home run against the Montreal Expos landed halfway up section 48 in the left-field upper deck. It was never topped.
14. *The Sporting News*
15. *Sports Illustrated*. His leadoff home run held up as the game-winning run and he had two outstanding catches in the outfield to arguably prevent five runs.
16. 182 hits, 107 runs and 31 stolen bases
17. Win a Gold Glove Award.
18. The Houston Astros for Rich Chiles and Buddy Harris.
19. The St. Louis Cardinals
20. The Los Angeles Dodgers

Dwight Gooden

1. Where was Dwight Gooden born on November 16, 1964?
2. With what pick was Gooden selected in the first round of the 1982 draft?
3. How many strikeouts did Gooden have while playing for the Class-A Lynchburg Mets in 1983?
4. How many strikeouts did he have during his first season with the Mets in 1984?
5. Whose rookie strikeout record did he break?
6. How old was Gooden when he made his Major League debut?
7. What award did Gooden win only once, during his second season in 1985?
8. What statistical category did he lead the National League in that season, wins, ERA, or strikeouts?
9. Only two pitchers have thrown more innings since Gooden's 276 in 1985. Name them.
10. How many more 20-win seasons would he have after 1985?
11. In 1986 what did Gooden become the youngest pitcher to do?
12. Who led the National League in strikeouts and then beat Gooden in Game 1 of the National League Championship Series?
13. Before he played in the World Series in 1986 what "other" World Series did he play in?
14. Despite missing a third of the 1987 season due to a suspension, how many games did Gooden win?
15. When Gooden went 19–7 in 1990, which teammate topped him for the team lead in strikeouts?
16. What non-positive statistical thing did Gooden do for the first time in 1992?
17. Despite that, what year-end national award did he win?
18. After the Mets, how many different organizations did Gooden play for?

19. What did Gooden do only once during his career, against the Seattle Mariners on May 14, 1996?

20. With which team did Gooden notch his first postseason win?

Answers

1. Tampa, Florida
2. Fifth
3. 300 in 191 innings.
4. A career-high 276
5. Herb Score's rookie record of 245 in 1955.
6. 19
7. The Cy Young Award
8. All three. He had 24 wins, 268 strikeouts, and a 1.53 ERA.
9. Roger Clemens and Charlie Hough, both in 1987
10. None
11. Start an All-Star Game. He was 21 years, seven months and 30 days of age.
12. Mike Scott of the Houston Astros
13. The Little League World Series
14. 15
15. David Cone with 223
16. Have a losing season, 10–13.
17. A Silver Slugger Award
18. Four: The Yankees twice along with the Indians, Astros and Devil Rays.
19. Throw a no-hitter.
20. He never won one, going 0–4 in 12 postseason appearances.

Davey Johnson

1. Which four Major League teams was Johnson with as a player?
2. How many All-Star Games did he play in?
3. How many Gold Gloves did he win?
4. While getting his first World Series ring in 1966 he was the last player to get a hit off which legendary pitcher?
5. How did Mets fans best know Johnson before he was hired as the team's manager?
6. What was he the first Major League player to do during the 1978 season?
7. What was the first team he managed?
8. What was the second team he managed?
9. How many consecutive losing seasons did the Mets have before Johnson took over in 1984?
10. What National League first did Johnson pull from 1984–88?
11. What was the Mets' worst showing in the National League East with Johnson at the helm?
12. How many games did the Mets win under Johnson?
13. Over 17 seasons how many games did Johnson win as a manager?
14. What was his team's record when Johnson was fired by the Mets in 1990?
15. In what statistical approach to baseball was he considered a pioneer?
16. Which international team did Johnson briefly coach in 2003 before Team USA?
17. How many other Major League teams did he manage?
18. Not including the three seasons there was a managerial change, leaving Johnson with a partial record, how many times did he have a losing record?
19. With which team was he named the league's Manager of the Year, and what year?
20. How many more World Series did he win after the Mets?

Answers

1. He played for the Baltimore Orioles (1965–72), Atlanta Braves (1973–75), Philadelphia Phillies (1977–78) and Chicago Cubs (1978). Johnson also had a two-year stint with the Yomiuri Giants (1975–76).
2. Four (1968–70, 1973)
3. Three (1969–71)
4. Sandy Koufax
5. He made the final out during the 1969 World Series.
6. Hit two grand slams as a pinch-hitter during one season.
7. The Miami Amigos of the AAA Inter-American League
8. The New York Mets' Class AA team, the Jackson Mets
9. Seven
10. He was the first National League manager to win at least 90 games in each of his first five seasons.
11. Second
12. .595
13. 1,372
14. 20–22
15. Sabermetrics
16. The Netherlands national team
17. Four: The Cincinnati Reds (1993–1995), Baltimore Orioles (1996–1997), Los Angeles Dodgers (1999–2000), and Washington Nationals (2011–2013).
18. Once, the 1999 Dodgers finished 77–85.
19. 2012 with the Nationals
20. None

Darryl Strawberry

1. Where was Darryl Strawberry born on March 12, 1962?
2. With what pick did the Mets select him in the 1980 draft?
3. In what round did his older brother Michael get selected during the same draft? (Bonus: Name the team)
4. In what year was he named the National League Rookie of the Year?
5. To how many consecutive All-Star Games was Strawberry named?
6. Who was Strawberry talking about when he said he would "bust that little redneck in the face"?
7. How many Silver Slugger Awards did Strawberry win?
8. Strawberry played what position 48 times with the Mets, but never with another team?
9. What did Strawberry do 75 times in right field, but not once in left field?
10. In what year did Strawberry lead the National League in home runs, and how many did he hit?
11. In what year was Strawberry named the Home Run Derby co-champion?
12. During his final season with the Mets in what place did Strawberry finish in MVP voting?
13. When Strawberry left the Mets, how big of a free-agent contract did Strawberry receive with the Dodgers?
14. In an effort to restart his career, which non-Major League team did Strawberry sign with on May 3, 1996?
15. How many 100-RBI seasons did Strawberry have?
16. Strawberry retired as the Mets' all-time leader in home runs. How many did he hit?
17. How many home runs did he hit over the nine seasons after he left the Mets?

18. Strawberry is one of three players in Major League history to play for the four current or former New York teams: the Dodgers, Giants, Mets, and Yankees. Name the other two.
19. In 1998, what was Strawberry the first player in American League history to do twice during one season?
20. On what show did Strawberry appear as a guest star in 1992 and allegedly cry?
21. What's the name of his memoir, published in 2009?
22. How many multi–home run games did Strawberry have with the Mets?

Darryl Strawberry, Mookie Wilson, and Cleon Jones throw out the first pitch at Game 5 of the 2015 World Series. (Cal Sport Media)

Answers

1. Los Angeles, California
2. First overall
3. 31st round by the Dodgers
4. 1983
5. Eight
6. Teammate Wally Backman
7. Two (1988 and 1990)
8. Center field
9. Record an assist
10. 1988. He hit 39 home runs.
11. 1986
12. Third
13. Five years, $22.25 million
14. The St. Paul Saints
15. Three, all with the Mets: 1987, 1988, and 1990. In 1991 he finished with 99 with the Dodgers.
16. 252
17. 83
18. Jose Vizcaino and Ricky Ledee. However, Strawberry is the only one of the three to play his entire career with those four teams.
19. Hit two pinch-hit grand slams.
20. *The Simpsons*, on the episode "Homer at the Bat."
21. *Straw: Finding My Way*
22. 22

John Franco

1. Where was John Anthony Franco born on September 17, 1960?
2. Where did he go to college?
3. How would Franco honor his father when he pitched?
4. Which team selected Franco in the fifth round of the 1981 draft?
5. With which team did he make his Major League debut on April 24, 1984?
6. Who had he been traded for in 1983?
7. What major award did he win for the first time in 1988?
8. How many times had Franco been named an All-Star when he joined the Mets?
9. Who were the three other players involved in the trade to bring Franco to the Mets on December 6, 1989?
10. How many times did Franco lead the National League in saves with the Mets?
11. What happened to Franco on May 1, 1996, when the Mets celebrated his 300th career save with "John Franco Day" at Shea Stadium?
12. What did Franco do for the first time in 1999?
13. Which number was greater, Franco's postseason wins or postseason saves?
14. What was his postseason ERA?
15. With which team did Franco play his final Major League game?
16. How old was he at the time?
17. How many saves did Franco have with the Mets?
18. How many saves did he have during his career?
19. As of 2015, who are the only three pitchers in Major League history to have more saves?
20. Which of them was a lefty like Franco?
21. What National League record did Franco set the moment he retired?

Answers

1. Brooklyn
2. St. John's University
3. He wore a shirt from where his father worked, the New York City Department of Sanitation, under his jersey.
4. The Los Angeles Dodgers
5. The Cincinnati Reds
6. Franco and Brett Wise were traded for Rafael Landestoy, who batted under .200 before retiring the following year.
7. The National League Rolaids Relief Man of the Year. He also won in 1990 after his first season with the Mets.
8. Three (1986, 1987, and 1989)
9. Franco was traded with Don Brown for Randy Myers and Kip Gross.
10. Two: 1990 and 1994
11. He was ejected in the fifth inning along with eight players after a brawl broke out against the Chicago Cubs.
12. Pitch in the postseason
13. Two wins compared to one save.
14. 1.88 in 15 appearances
15. The Houston Astros
16. 44
17. 276
18. 424
19. Mariano Rivera, Trevor Hoffman, and Lee Smith.
20. None of them. Franco is the all-time saves leader among left-handed pitchers.
21. 1,119 games pitched, the most in National League history and third most in Major League history.

Mike Piazza

1. Where was Mike Piazza raised?
2. Who once gave him personal instruction in his backyard batting cage when Piazza was 12?
3. Where did he play college baseball?
4. Why did the Los Angeles Dodgers select him in the 62nd round of the 1988 draft?
5. What big change did the Dodgers ask him to make?
6. How many home runs did Piazza hit as a rookie in 1993?
7. How many consecutive appearances in the All-Star Game did he make starting that same year?
8. With which two pitchers did he catch no-hitters?
9. Who all was involved in the mega-deal between the Los Angeles Dodgers and Florida Marlins on May 15, 1998?
10. How many games did Piazza play for the Marlins before he was traded to the Mets?
11. How many times was Piazza named the league's Most Valuable Player?
12. In what statistical category did Piazza lead the Major Leagues with four in 1998?
13. Where did he hit the longest home run in that stadium's history, and where was he just one of three players to hit a home run completely out of the stadium?
14. How long of a standing ovation did Piazza receive during his final game in a Mets uniform on October 2, 2005?
15. Who did Piazza hit a home run off of on August 9, 2006, resulting in a rare curtain call for a visiting player?
16. With which team did Piazza play his last Major League game?
17. How many times did he hit at least 30 home runs in a season?

18. How many Silver Slugger awards did Piazza win?
19. Which country did Piazza play for during the 2006 World Baseball Classic?
20. What special honor was Piazza given on September 28, 2008?

Answers

1. Phoenixville, Pennsylvania, just outside of Philadelphia.
2. Ted Williams
3. Miami-Dade Community College
4. Dodgers manager Tommy Lasorda was a childhood friend of Piazza's father, Vince, and the godfather of the slugger's youngest brother, Tommy. Vince asked Lasorda to draft Mike as a personal favor.
5. Lasorda asked Piazza to give up his first base position and learn how to catch in order to improve his chances of reaching the major leagues. He also had him attend a special training camp for catchers in the Dominican Republic.
6. 35, the most ever by a rookie catcher. He was named the National League Rookie of the Year.
7. 10. He played in 12 All-Star Games overall.
8. Ramon Martinez and Hideo Nomo
9. Mike Piazza and Todd Zeile went to the Marlins in return for Gary Sheffield, Charles Johnson, Bobby Bonilla, Manuel Barrios, and Jim Eisenreich.
10. Five
11. Zero. In 1996 he finished second San Diego's Ken Caminiti after batting .336 with 36 home runs, 105 RBIs, 87 runs and 16 doubles. Caminiti later admitted to taking steroids during his award-winning season.
12. Grand slams
13. He had the longest home run ever hit at the Astrodome in Houston, and is one of three players to completely hit one out of Dodger Stadium over the leftfield pavilion.
14. 8 minutes.
15. Pedro Martinez. Piazza responded by hitting another home run in his subsequent at-bat.
16. The Oakland Athletics
17. Nine, including eight straight (1995–2002).
18. 10
19. Italy. He is of Italian and Slovakian ancestry.
20. During the "Shea Goodbye" ceremony Piazza received the final pitch in the history of the stadium from Tom Seaver. They then walked off the field together via the center field exit to close the stadium. On April 13, 2009, they reunited for the first-pitch ceremony at Citi Field.

David Wright

1. Where was David Allen Wright born on December 20, 1982?
2. In what round did the Mets take Wright in the 2001 draft?
3. How did the Mets have that pick?
4. Where had Wright planned to attend college?
5. Against which team did Wright make his Major League debut on July 21, 2004?
6. What was his first Major League hit and who was it against?
7. In what negative category did Wright tie for the Major League lead in 2005?
8. On August 9, 2005, who did Wright retire with a over-the-shoulder barehanded catch that resulted in a standing ovation even with the Mets playing on the road?
9. What two awards did Wright win in back-to-back seasons, 2007–08?
10. What exclusive club did Wright join on September 16, 2007?
11. What first did Wright do on April 13, 2009?
12. What scare did Wright experience on August 15, 2009, which contributed to a sub-par season?
13. After arriving early to spring training, how did Wright start the 2010 season?
14. What career first did Wright experience on August 7, 2011?
15. In which category does Wright hold the franchise record: RBIs, doubles, total bases, runs scored, walks, sacrifice flies, times on base, extra base hits, strikeouts, or hits?
16. What "second" (the first being in 2006) did Wright experience at the end of the 2015 regular season?
17. Due to what trade in 2015 did Wright become the longest-tenured active player to have played his entire career with one team?
18. What medical condition was he diagnosed with in 2015?

19. Where was David Wright invited to have dinner along with other Major League players on February 5, 2007?

20. More than 140 players have appeared at third base for the Mets since 1962, but Wright is one of only six to have appeared in as many as 300. Name the other five.

David Wright rips a double in Game 3 of the 2015 NLCS against the Cubs. (Robin Alam/Icon Sportswire)

Answers

1. Norfolk, Virginia
2. First. He was the 38th-overall selection.
3. It was compensation for the Mets losing Mike Hampton to the Colorado Rockies in free agency.
4. Georgia Tech to study engineering.
5. The Montreal Expos
6. A double off Zach Day
7. Errors by a third baseman. He had 24.
8. Brian Giles of the San Diego Padres
9. Both the Gold Glove and Silver Slugger awards for National League third basemen
10. The 30-30 club (30 home runs and 30 stolen bases)
11. He hit the first home run during the opening game at Citi Field.
12. He was hit in the head with a 93 mph fastball by San Francisco Giants pitcher Matt Cain.
13. He hit a two-run home run on his first at-bat of the season, off the Florida Marlins' Josh Johnson.
14. He played shortstop due to injuries to José Reyes (hamstring) and Daniel Murphy (knee).
15. Actually he holds the franchise record in all of those statistical categories.
16. He played in the playoffs.
17. Chase Utley's August trade from the Philadelphia Phillies to the Los Angeles Dodgers.
18. Spinal stenosis
19. The White House by President George W. Bush.
20. Howard Johnson (835), Wayne Garrett (729), Hubie Brooks (516), Edgardo Alfonzo (515), and Robin Ventura (441).

Seven

Jersey Numbers

There are only four numbers that will never be worn again by anyone on the New York Mets, and one of them was Jackie Robinson's No. 42, which was retired in all of baseball in 1997.

As of 2015, the only Mets pitcher to have his number retired was Tom Seaver, which was done during a special tribute at Shea Stadium on June 24, 1988.

Gil Hodges, the manager of the Miracle Mets, had his No. 14 jersey retired on June 9, 1973. His teams went 339–309 from 1968–1971, and he also played two seasons with the Mets (1962–63).

However the number that may be best associated with the Mets is 37, which was worn by its fist manager, Casey Stengel. He might have won seven World Series managing the New York Yankees, but his four long seasons with the expansion club, when his teams were a horrendous 175–404, endeared him to Mets fans forever.

Stengel's jersey was retired on September 2, 1965, before he was elected to the Baseball Hall of Fame.

Jersey Numbers

Give the number for the following:

1. Bobby Valentine as a player
2. Mookie Wilson
3. Ron Hunt
4. Jerry Grote
5. Darryl Strawberry
6. Dave Kingman
7. Jerry Koosman
8. Mike Piazza
9. Joe Pignanto
10. Rogers Hornsby
11. Johan Santana
12. Orel Hershiser
13. Mo Vaughn
14. Name the only two players who wore Gil Hodges' number before he did?
15. Duke Snider
16. Yogi Berra
17. Ron Gardenhire
18. Dave Magadan
19. Frank Viola
20. Who is the only player in Mets' history to wear 00?
21. What two players have worn 0?
22. Who wore 99?
23. Garth Brooks in Spring Training.
24. Who was the last player to wear No. 42 for the Mets?
25. Through 2015 which number has been worn by the most different players?

Answers

1. 1
2. 1
3. 33
4. 15
5. 18
6. 26
7. 36
8. 31
9. 52
10. 53
11. 57
12. 55
13. 42
14. Ken Boyer (1966–67) and Ron Swoboda (1965)
15. 4
16. 8
17. 19
18. 29
19. He also wore 29.
20. Tony Clark
21. Terry McDaniel (1992) and Rey Ordonez (1996–1997)
22. Turk Wendell (1997–2001)
23. 1
24. Mo Vaughn
25. No. 6, 40 different players have worn it, but usually for only one or two seasons. Wally Backman had it the longest from 1981–88.

Eight

The Records

If anyone wants to know what kind of presence David Wright had on the New York Mets all they have to do is go back to the night of August 24, 2015.

The Mets were visiting the Philadelphia Phillies when Wright was activated off the 60-day disabled list, where he had been since April 15 after straining his hamstring sliding into second base against the same Phillies.

He was later diagnosed with spinal stenosis in his lumbar spine, which is the narrowing of the spinal column in the lower back.

Despite that, Wright crushed the third pitch he saw for a solo home run.

He was then followed by basically everyone in the Mets lineup.

Juan Lagares added a solo shot in the third inning, Wilmer Flores went back-to-back with Travis d'Arnaud in the fourth and hit a go-ahead, three-run home run in the fifth. Michael Cuddyer went deep two batters later, Daniel Murphy tied the franchise record with a two-run shot in the sixth and Yoenis Cespedes topped it off with a two-run blast in the ninth inning.

"I guess I said it when Cespedes hit his home run, you look at each other and just go, 'Wow,'" manager Terry Collins told MLB.com. "The power has all of a sudden kicked in."

Overall, the Mets hit a franchise-record eight home runs during their 16–7 victory at Citizens Bank Park. They also set a club record with 15 extra-base hits (eight home runs, seven doubles), which according to the Elias Sports Bureau tied for the third-highest total in Major League history.

How's that for a welcome back?

The Records

1. Who holds the franchise record for longest hitting streak?
2. Who set the Mets' record for the most hits in consecutive official at-bats with nine in 1996?
3. Who tied it three years later?
4. Who was the opponent when the Mets set the team record with 23 runs scored in a single game on August 16, 1987?
5. Who was the opponent when the Mets set the team record with 28 hits in a single game on July 4, 1985? (Bonus if you can name how many innings the game went.)
6. Who had 19 outfield assists in 1974?
7. What three outfielders finished one short of that mark?
8. Who holds the franchise record for hits by a pitcher over a single season?
9. Who holds the Mets record for home runs allowed over a career?
10. Who holds the team record for home runs allowed over a season?
11. Who has hit the most home runs among opposing players?
12. How many saves did Francisco Rodriguez have to set a Major League record in 2008?
13. What's the club record for consecutive shutout innings? (Hint: Think Douglas Adams.)
14. What's the Mets record for consecutive scoreless innings? (Hint: Think almost Douglas Adams.)

15. Who has hit the most grand slams as a Met?
16. Which two players are tied for the most home runs in a single month for the Mets?
17. Who holds the team record for home runs in extra innings?
18. When Tom Seaver set a Major League record by striking out 19 San Diego Padres on April 22, 1970, how many in a row did he fan at the end of the game?
19. Who did Dwight Gooden replace as the youngest 20-game winner in baseball history?
20. Which player holds the franchise record for walks in a game?

August 24, 2015: David Wright greets Daniel Murphy after yet another home run. (Icon Sportswire)

Answers

1. Moises Alou, 30 games in 2007.
2. Jose Vizcaino
3. John Olerud
4. The Chicago Cubs
5. The Atlanta Braves (19 innings)
6. Rusty Staub with 19 in 1974.
7. Joel Youngblood, Kevin McReynolds, and Bernard Gilkey
8. Dwight Gooden with 21 in 1985
9. Tom Seaver with 212
10. Roger Craig with 35 in 1962
11. Willie Stargell with 60
12. 62
13. 42 by the 1969 World Champions from September 23–28. To quote the Mets media guide: "Included in that streak were six shutout frames vs. St. Louis on the 23rd, a complete game victory by Gary Gentry over the Cards on the 24th, complete game wins by Jerry Koosman and Tom Seaver at Philadelphia on the 26th and 27th and a 2–0 victory over the Phillies on the 28th.
14. 39, from September 11–15, 1963
15. Mike Piazza with six
16. Dave Kingman (July 1975) and Gary Carter (September 1985) with 13
17. Howard Johnson with nine
18. He struck out the last 10 batters he faced. No one has done that since.
19. Bob Feller in 1939
20. Vince Coleman with five (August 10, 1992 vs. Pittsburgh)

Nine

Quotes

With all due respect to Yogi Berra, who died at the age of 90 in 2015, when it comes to being a quote machine about New York baseball, no one could top Casey Stengel.

One of baseball's true characters was the first manager in New York Mets history and he was one of the few things that kept people coming back to the ballpark, reporters included.

Some of his comments about that 1962 team included:

"Can't anybody here play this game?"

"We've got to learn to stay out of triple plays."

"When I go back in my mind to our play in 1962 I just wonder how we ever got to win 40 games."

But Stengel, who was on the winning side in eight World Series, including seven as a manager, knew baseball as well.

For example, on his three catchers he said: "I got one that can throw but can't catch, one that can catch but can't throw, and one who can hit but can't do either."

Regarding rookies Ed Kranepool and Greg Goossen in 1965, he said: "See that fellow over there? He's 20 years old. In 10 years he has a chance to be a star. Now, that fellow over there, he's 20, too. In 10 years he has a chance to be 30."

Kranepool played 18 years with the Mets while Goossen did in fact turn 30, five years after his last game in the major leagues.

Quotes

Who said the following quotes:

1. "The Mets have shown me more ways to lose than I even knew existed."
2. "I wasn't going to make the last out of the World Series."
3. "If the Mets can win the World Series, the United States can get out of Vietnam."
4. "He made the Big Red Machine look like me hitting today."
5. "I did not want to leave the Mets and I did not want to leave New York."
6. "We're a young team. We're just coming. We all played together last year and we're together again this year. When you play together a few years, you get to know each other and things improve. Yes sir, there's a different feeling on the team this year. There's more togetherness. There's more pride. We're a close-knit team."
7. "I'm probably the only guy who worked for [Casey] Stengel before and after he was a genius."
8. "Ya Gotta Believe!"
9. "It ain't over 'til it's over" and "We were overwhelming underdogs."
10. "[Gil Hodges' death] absolutely shattered me. I just flew apart. I didn't leave my apartment in Texas for three days. I didn't want to see anybody. I couldn't get myself to the funeral. It was like I'd lost a part of my family."
11. "I am certainly happy that I don't have to run for election against Gary Carter."
12. "I'm glad I don't have to face that guy every day. He has that look that few hitters have. I don't know if it is in his stance, his eyes or what. But you can tell he means business."
13. "The same way as to anybody else, except don't let the ball go."
14. "There's no reason for what goes on around here. But there isn't anything I can do about it. I just work here."
15. "Well, then I think you are doing a lousy job."

16. "I wasn't the ugly American there that I am here."

17. "We actually like their team. Well, at least 24 of the guys."

18. "Maybe I'm just a late bloomer. There are still people out there saying, 'Maybe he's a fluke.' I know I'm not a fluke. I know I can pitch here."

19. "He had Whitey Ford's stuff and Edsel Ford's luck."

20. "We've had him three full seasons and although he's a hell of a prospect, he hasn't done it for us. How long can you wait?"

21. "For me, I was always a Met at heart."

22. "Rule #1, you don't make the third out at third base with Mike Piazza coming up."

23. "The reason we won was him. He made us all better."

24. "You're next!"

25. "My wife wanted a big diamond."

26. "I wanted to get people's attention. There are always tons of reporters here when something bad is happening. I don't like a lot of them...What are they going to do? Fine me?"

27. "I know you are all gonna try, but you're not going to be able to wipe this smile off my face."

28. "I dunno. I never smoked any Astroturf. "

29. "There will be two buses to the park from the hotel. The two o'clock bus is for those who need a little extra work. Then there will be an empty bus leaving at five o'clock."

30. "Baseball is like church. Many attend, but few understand."

Answers

1. Casey Stengel
2. Gary Carter
3. Tom Seaver
4. Bud Harrelson. The comment about teammate Jon Matlack sparked the brawl in the 1973 National League Championship Series.
5. Al Leiter
6. Jim Grote before the 1969 season
7. Warren Spahn, who briefly played under Stengel for the 1942 Braves and the 1965 Mets.
8. Tug McGraw. It became the rallying call for the 1973 playoff team.
9. Yogi Berra about the 1973 Mets
10. Don Drysdale
11. Pierre Elliott Trudeau when he was prime minister of Canada
12. Dwight Gooden on Don Mattingly after facing him in a 1989 spring training game.
13. Tug McGraw on the best way to pitch to Hank Aaron.
14. Brian McRae on the Mets and manager Bobby Valentine.
15. Cleon Jones when he asked an umpire if he could get thrown out of a game for thinking, and the umpire said 'No.'
16. Bobby Valentine on managing the Chiba Lotte Marines in Japan's Pacific League.
17. Todd Pratt on the New York Yankees and Roger Clemens before the 2000 World Series.
18. Rick Reed
19. Richie Ashburn on teammate Ken MacKenzie.
20. Mets general manager Bob Scheffing on trading Nolan Ryan.
21. Dwight Gooden
22. Bobby Valentine
23. Bud Harrelson on Gil Hodges and the 1969 Mets.
24. Darryl Strawberry reportedly said it to Gary Carter after getting into a scuffle with Keith Hernandez during a spring training team photo shoot in 1989.
25. Mookie Wilson on why he got married on a baseball field.
26. Bret Saberhagen while admitting to lighting a firecracker and throwing it under a table near reporters in the Shea Stadium clubhouse on July 7, 1993.
27. Bobby Bonilla after signing a $29 million contract with the Mets.
28. Tug McGraw after being asked if he preferred natural grass to artificial turf.
29. Casey Stengel
30. Manager Wes Westrum

Ten

More Than 50 Years, More Than 50 Questions

In 2012 the New York Mets celebrated their 50th anniversary with a series of special events ranging from Tom Seaver bobblehead night to a special "Banner Day" at Citi Field.

Of course, an all-time Mets team was announced, even though the selections were for the most part pretty obvious.

C: Mike Piazza
1B: Keith Hernandez
2B: Edgardo Alfonzo
SS: Jose Reyes
3B: David Wright
LF: Cleon Jones
CF: Carlos Beltran
RF: Darryl Strawberry
RHP: Tom Seaver
LHP: Jerry Koosman
LHRP: Tug McGraw
RHRP: Roger McDowell
Manager: Davey Johnson

More Than 50 Years

Here's a question for every season of New York Mets baseball:

1962: Who went 10–24 as a starting pitcher during the Mets' inaugural season?

1963: Who started an all-rookie lineup against the Mets on September 27?

1964: Who threw the National League's first perfect game since 1880 against the Mets at Shea Stadium on Father's Day?

1965: True or false, the Mets didn't lose 100 games for the first time in their existence?

1966: For the first time the Mets didn't finish last in the National League. Which team did?

1967: During the second game of a June 11th doubleheader, the Mets and what opponent combined to tie a Major League record with 11 home runs? (Bonus: Name the teams that set the mark in 1950)

1968: What team statistic did the Mets lead the National League in, which showed a lot of promise for their immediate future?

1969: What impressive win-total milestone did the Mets reach for the first time while winning the first National League East Division title?

1970: The Mets had three starting pitchers win at least 10 games. Name them.

1971: Who had a career-best 11 wins along with a 1.70 ERA and 109 strikeouts?

1972: Although he didn't know it at the time, which Mets pitcher gave up the final hit of Roberto Clemente's career, which happened to be No. 3,000, on September 30th?

1973: While playing for the Mets, who did Willie Mays hit his final career home run against?

1974: Who did the Mets lose to 4–3 in 25 innings, in a game which included

175 official at-bats, setting a Major League record with 45 runners left on base, and ended at 3:13 am?

1975: What future manager tied a Major League record by hitting into four consecutive double plays during a 6–2 loss to the Houston Astros?

1976: Who had six shutouts en route to a 17–10 record?

1977: With career strikeout No. 2,397, during an 8–0 victory against the Reds, who did Tom Seaver pass on the all-time strikeouts list?

1978: Who had the National League's best ERA at 2.43?

1979: What stigma did the Mets narrowly avoid by winning their last six games?

1980: Who led the Mets in home runs (16), RBIs (76) and hits (162)?

1981: How tall was Dave Kingman?

1982: Who, thanks to a trade, became the first player to hit safely in two different cities, for two different teams on the same day?

1983: True or false, the Mets finished with the worst record in the major leagues?

1984: When Dwight Gooden struck out 276 batters he not only topped the National League but set a Major League record for a rookie. Whose record did he break?

1985: Who wrote the famous *Sports Illustrated* story about Mets super-prospect Sidd Finch, who could throw a baseball 168 mph?

1986: When Commissioner Peter Ueberroth publicly suspended seven prominent players for drug abuse in hopes of setting an example, which one was a New York Met?

1987: Who were the first teammates to join the 30/30 club (30 home runs and 30 stolen base) during the same season?

1988: Who went 20–3 to lead the National League in winning percentage at .870?

1989: Who with a home run on August 20 became just the third two-time member of the 30/30 club along with Bobby Bonds and Willie Mays?

1990: Who led the National League with a .425 on-base percentage?

1991: Who led the National League with 38 home runs and 117 RBIs?

1992:   What record of Mickey Mantle's did Eddie Murray break during a 15–1 victory over the Pittsburgh Pirates?

1993:   Which number was bigger, wins or how many millions made up the team payroll?

1994:   Who gave up three home runs on consecutive at-bats to Tuffy Rhodes of the Cubs on Opening Day?

1995:   Who led the Mets in strikeouts with 209, but posted a 10–10 record?

1996:   Who recorded his 300th save exactly 12 years after recording his first while with the Cincinnati Reds?

1997:   Who, after winning just nine games during his first nine seasons in the major leagues, won 13 for the Mets?

1998:   Who led the Mets with 93 RBIs?

1999:   Who stole 37 bases while appearing in 116 games for the Mets?

2000:   Where did the Mets open the season, and which team did it face in the first regular season game ever played outside of North America?

2001:   Who led the Mets with 11 wins, Kevin Appier, Al Leiter, or Steve Trachsel?

2002:   Despite having the biggest payroll in the National League East, what team record in futility did the Mets set?

2003:   The only team to finish worse than the Mets in the National League was the San Diego Padres. What was the difference in their payrolls?

2004:   Who led the Mets with 30 home runs and 76 RBIs?

2005:   What record did Mike Piazza extend during his final season with the Mets?

2006:   Who hit for the cycle on June 21?

2007:   With the Mets seeing their seven game lead evaporate over the last 18 days of the regular season, which team finished atop the National League East?

2008:   What pitcher led the National League in appearances with 86?

2009:   Who became the 25th member of the 500 home run club on April 17th?

2010:   Which struggling franchise matched the 1963 Mets for the worst road record in a 162-game season at 17–64?

2011: Who did the Mets defeat 10–9 on July 28th to pull off the first four-game sweep in that franchise's history?

2012: Who led the National League with five complete games and three shutouts, which both exceeded his previous career totals, and struck out 230 batters when his previous best was 134?

2013: Which rival did the Mets sweep for the first time in a series?

2014: Who had his insignia on the Mets' alternate home and road jerseys?

2015: Who became the first player in major league history to record at least five hits in a game with three home runs including a grand slam?

Answers

1962: Roger Craig

1963: The Houston Colt 45s, specifically manager Harry Craft

1964: Jim Bunning of the Philadelphia Phillies

1965: False, they lost 112

1966: The Chicago Cubs finished 59–103, while the Mets were 66–95.

1967: The Chicago Cubs. The Detroit Tigers and New York Yankees first did it.

1968: Fewest hits allowed

1969: 100 wins

1970: Tom Seaver (18), Jerry Koosman (12), and Jim McAndrew (10)

1971: Tug McGraw

1972: John Matlack

1973: Don Gullet of the Cincinnati Reds

1974: The St. Louis Cardinals

1975: Joe Torre. He tied "Goose" Goslin (1934) and Mike Kreevich (1939)

1976: Jon Matlack

1977: Sandy Koufax

1978: Craig Swan

1979: 100 losses. The Mets finished 63–99.

1980: Lee Mazzilli

1981: 6'6"

1982: On August 4, Joel Youngblood hit a two-run single off Fergie Jenkins for the Mets in Chicago. That evening he hit a single off Steve Carlton for the Expos in Philadelphia. Both pitchers ended up in the Hall of Fame.

1983: False, but they were close. The Seattle Mariners finished 60–102, while the Mets had the worst record in the National League at 68–94.

1984: Herb Score with 245

1985: George Plimpton. It took some fans a while to realize that the April 1 story about a pitching Tibetan Buddhist was really an April Fool's Day joke.
1986: Keith Hernandez
1987: Howard Johnson and Darryl Strawberry
1988: David Cone
1989: Howard Johnson
1990: Dave Magadan
1991: Howard Johnson
1992: Most RBIs by a switch-hitter (1,510)
1993: Wins. The Mets had 59, compared to the payroll of $40.8 million.
1994: Dwight Gooden. The Mets still won, 12–8.
1995: Bobby Jones
1996: John Franco
1997: Rick Reed
1998: John Olerud
1999: Ricky Henderson
2000: The Tokyo Dome in Japan, marking the first Major League game ever played on Asian soil. The Cubs beat the Mets, 5–3.
2001: Actually, they all had 11 wins. No one else had more than eight.
2002: Most consecutive games lost at home during a single season with 15.
2003: Nearly $70 million. The Mets payroll was more than $117 million, while the Padres paid their team just under $48 million.
2004: Mike Cameron
2005: Career home runs by a catcher. At the time he had 376.
2006: Jose Reyes
2007: The Philadelphia Phillies
2008: Pedro Feliciano
2009: Gary Sheffield
2010: The Pittsburgh Pirates
2011: The Cincinnati Reds
2012: R.A. Dickey
2013: The New York Yankees
2014: The team mascot, Mr. Met
2015: Yoenis Cespedes at Colorado on August 21.

Eleven

Opening Day Lineups

When it comes to baseball trivia there's nothing like an Opening Day lineup.

It's when the newest players first appear, departures become more real and the changes over the offseason take hold. Among pitchers it's when the staff ace usually takes his rightful place and begins what's hopefully the long march toward the playoffs and a title.

For some reason, fans can remember and recite Opening Day lineups until their dying day even though it could look different with each passing game. More than an annual benchmark, it's like a progress report, and no one ever remembers who started the second game of a 162-game season.

Nevertheless, no one was better on Opening Day than Tom Seaver, who holds the record for Opening Day starts by a pitcher with 16. He holds the Mets' record of 11 straight starts, during which his record was 6–0. He made three Opening Day starts for the Cincinnati Reds and two for the Chicago White Sox.

From 1968 through 1983, the Mets' Opening Day starting pitchers went 16 consecutive years without a loss. During the 31-year period from 1968 through 1998, they only lost two games: Mike Torrez in 1984 and Dwight Gooden in 1990.

Opening Day Lineups

How many of these 15 seasons can you peg the Opening Day lineup?

1. 1962
2. 1968
3. 1969
4. 1970
5. 1973
6. 1981
7. 1985
8. 1986
9. 1988
10. 1994
11. 1995
12. 2000
13. 2003
14. 2006
15. 2015

The Marlins and Mets line up for introductions at Citi Field on Opening Day 2010. (Kathy Willens)

Answers

1. **1962**
   Richie Ashburn, CF
   Felix Mantilla, SS
   Charlie Neal, 2B
   Frank Thomas, LF
   Gus Bell, RF
   Gil Hodges, 1B
   Don Zimmer, 3B
   Hobie Landrith, C
   Roger Craig, P

2. **1968**
   Bud Harrelson, SS
   Ken Boswell, 2B
   Tommie Agee, CF
   Ron Swoboda, RF
   Ed Kranepool, 1B
   Art Shamsky, LF
   J.C. Martin, C
   Ed Charles, 3B
   Tom Seaver, P

3. **1969**
   Tommie Agee, CF
   Rod Gaspar, RF
   Ken Boswell, 2B
   Cleon Jones, LF
   Ed Charles, 3B
   Ed Kranepool, 1B
   Jerry Grote, C
   Bud Harrelson
   SS Tom Seaver, P

4. **1970**
   Tommie Agee, CF
   Ed Harrelson, SS
   Joe Foy, 3B
   Cleon Jones, LF
   Art Shamsky, 1B
   Ron Swoboda, RF
   Wayne Garrett, 2B
   Jerry Grote, C
   Tom Seaver, P

5. **1973**
   Bud Harrelson, SS
   Felix Millan, 2B
   Willie Mays, CF
   Rusty Staub, RF
   Cleon Jones, LF
   John Milner, 1B
   Jim Fregosi, 3B
   Duffy Dyer, C
   Tom Seaver, P

6. **1981**
   Mookie Wilson, RF
   Frank Taveras, SS
   Lee Mazzilli, CF
   Dave Kingman, LF
   Rusty Staub, 1B
   Alex Trevino, C
   Hubie Brooks, 3B
   Doug Flynn, 2B
   Pat Zachry, P

7. **1985**
   Wally Backman, 2B
   Mookie Wilson, CF
   Keith Hernandez, 1B
   Gary Carter, C
   Darryl Strawberry, RF
   George Foster, LF
   Howard Johnson, 3B
   Rafael Santana, SS
   Dwight Gooden, P

8. **1986**
   Lenny Dykstra, CF
   Wally Backman, 2B
   Keith Hernandez, 1B
   Gary Carter, C
   Darryl Strawberry, RF
   George Foster, LF
   Howard Johnson, 3B
   Rafael Santana, SS
   Dwight Gooden, P

9. **1988**
   Lenny Dykstra, CF
   Tim Teufel, 2B
   Keith Hernandez, 1B
   Darryl Strawberry, RF
   Kevin McReynolds, LF
   Gary Carter, C
   Howard Johnson, 3B
   Kevin Elster, SS
   Dwight Gooden, P

10. **1994**
    Jose Vizcaino, SS
    Todd Hundley, C
    Kevin McReynolds, LF
    Bobby Bonilla, 3B
    Jeff Kent, 2B
    David Segui, 1B
    Jeromy Burnitz, RF
    Ryan Thompson, CF
    Dwight Gooden, P

11. **1995**
    Brett Butler, CF
    Jose Vizcaino, SS
    Rico Brogna, 1B
    Bobby Bonilla, 3B
    Jeff Kent, 2B
    David Segui, LF
    Carl Everett, RF
    Todd Hundley, C
    Bobby J. Jones, P

12. **2000**
    Rickey Henderson, LF
    Darryl Hamilton, CF
    Edgardo Alfonzo, 2B
    Mike Piazza, C
    Robin Ventura, 3B
    Jay Bell, RF
    Todd Zeile, 1B
    Rey Ordoñez, SS
    Mike Hampton, P

13. **2003**
    Roger Cedeño, CF
    Roberto Alomar, 2B
    Cliff Floyd, LF
    Mike Piazza, C
    Mo Vaughn, 1B
    Ty Wigginton, 3B
    Jeromy Burnitz, RF
    Rey Sanchez, SS
    Tom Glavine, P

14. **2006**
    Jose Reyes, SS
    Paul Lo Duca, C
    Carlos Beltran, CF
    Carlos Delgado, 1B
    David Wright, 3B
    Cliff Floyd, LF
    Xavier Nady, RF
    Anderson Hernandez, 2B
    Tom Glavine, P

15. **2015**
    Curtis Granderson, RF
    David Wright, 3B
    Lucas Duda, 1B
    Michael Cuddyer , LF
    Daniel Murphy, 2B
    Juan Lagares, CF
    Travis d'Arnaud, C
    Wilmer Flores, SS
    Bartolo Colon, RHP

Twelve

Drafts, Trades, and Free Agency, Oh My!

For the record the first player the New York Mets selected the initial amateur draft in 1965 was Les Rohr, a right-handed pitcher who played one year in the minors and was then called up to the parent team.

Unfortunately for the Mets, who had used the second-overall selection on him, Rohr lasted two years (he was called up September 19th,1967, and released that same day in 1969) and had a career record of 2–3.

The subsequent year the Mets had the first-overall pick and selected Steven Chilcott, a catcher from Lancaster, California, who sustained a shoulder injury from which he never fully recovered. He played seven years in the minors and is one of three players to be picked first overall in the MLB draft to never reach the major leagues, the other two being Brien Taylor and Matt Bush.

Of course, not all Mets draft picks have been busts, far from it.

Four first-round picks have won championships with the franchise. Outfielders Lee Mazzilli (1973) and Darryl Strawberry (1980), infielder Wally Backman (1977), and pitcher Dwight Gooden (1982) all played in the 1986 World Series for the Mets' second championship team.

No first-round picks were on the 1969 title team.

Three first-round picks have gone on to win the Rookie of the Year Award with the Mets: Jon Matlack in 1972, Strawberry in 1983, and Gooden in 1984. Gooden also won the Cy Young Award in 1985.

Drafts, Trades, and Free Agency

1. Who did the Mets get in exchange for Tom Seaver on June 15, 1977?
2. What place did the Mets finish in the standings in each of the three years after trading Seaver?
3. What did the Mets give up to re-acquire Seaver on December 16, 1982?
4. In 1984 how did the Mets lose Seaver for a second time?
5. With Seaver's departure, who did it open a roster spot for?
6. Who shot down a potential trade to acquire Seaver from the Chicago White Sox in 1985?
7. Instead, who was Seaver traded for during the 1986 season?
8. Who did the Mets give up to acquire John Olerud from the Toronto Blue Jays on December 20, 1996?
9. What did the Mets give up to the Minnesota Twins to acquire left-handed pitcher Johan Santana on February 2, 2008?
10. How did the Mets acquire David Wright?
11. Who was the Mets' first first-round draft pick in 1965?
12. The Mets have had the first-overall selection in the draft five times. Who did they pick?
13. On May 9, 1962, the first Met was traded along with some cash to the Baltimore Orioles. Who was acquired?
14. Who did the Mets trade Nolan Ryan and three other players to California for?

15. Which two players did the Mets trade to St. Louis in acquiring Keith Hernandez in 1983?

16. Who did the Mets give up in exchange for Mike Piazza from the Florida Marlins?

17. Who did the Mets and Yankees swap on December 7, 2001?

18. After being traded away from the Mets, who ended up playing for the Los Angeles Dodgers, Cleveland Indians, Milwaukee Brewers, Baltimore Orioles, St. Louis Cardinals, San Diego Padres, New York Yankees, and Minnesota Twins?

19. Who did the Mets give up to acquire Rusty Staub from the Montreal Expos?

20. On June 18, 1989, who did the Mets give up to acquire second baseman Juan Samuel?

Keith Hernandez launches a home run during his days with the Cardinals.

Answers

1. Pat Zachry, Steve Henderson, Doug Flynn, and Dan Norman from the Cincinnati Reds
2. Last
3. Charlie Puleo, Lloyd McClendon and Jason Felice
4. He was claimed in a free-agent compensation draft by the Chicago White Sox.
5. Dwight Gooden
6. Manager Davey Johnson
7. Steve Lyons
8. Robert Person
9. Carlos Gomez (OF), Philip Humber (RHP), and minor leaguers Kevin Mulvey (RHP) and Deolis Guerra (RHP).
10. The Mets selected him in the first round (38th pick overall) of the 2001 First Year Player Draft.
11. Left-handed pitcher Les Rohr
12. C Steve Chilcott, 1966; INF Tim Foli, 1968; OF Darryl Strawberry, 1980; OF Shawn Abner, 1984; RHP Paul Wilson, 1994.
13. Marv Throneberry
14. Jim Fregosi
15. Neil Allen and Rick Ownbey
16. Preston Wilson, Ed Yarnell, and Geoff Goetz
17. The Mets traded Robin Ventura for David Justice.
18. Reliever Jesse Orosco
19. First baseman-outfielder Mike Jorgensen, shortstop Tim Foli, and outfielder Ken Singleton.
20. Lenny Dkystra, Roger McDowell, and Tom Edens to Philadelphia.

Thirteen

The Miracle Mets

Before moving on to the postseason section of this book it seems only fitting to include a special look at the 1969 team that became known as the "Miracle Mets," or "Amazin' Mets."

To quote *Life* magazine when it recently looked back on that historic team:

"The 1969 New York Mets were, in one respect, like a lot of other phenomena from that long-ago, undead decade: even people who weren't yet born "remember" that championship team, in much the same way they "remember" Woodstock, the moon landing, MLK's assassination, Altamont, the release of The White Album, and other cultural and political touchstones of the era.

"The '69 'Amazin' Mets' of Seaver, Clendennon, Koosman, Kranepool, Jones, Agee, Grote, and the rest are part of pop-culture lore as surely as Electric Ladyland and the police riots at the Democratic convention in Chicago in 1968—not because they were the most dominant team of the age, but precisely because they weren't. They were the Bad News Bears of the majors . . . except that, in the Mets' case, they actually won it all in the end."

The Miracle Mets

1. What was the Mets record the year before, 1968?
2. What was the highest the team had previously finished in the National League standings?
3. In what month did the Mets have a losing record?
4. Previously, what was the longest the Mets had been over .500 into a season?
5. What was the team's record at the quarter mark of the season (41 games)?
6. Which opponent swept the Mets twice in the middle of the season?
7. What negative Major League record did the Mets set while defeating the St. Louis Cardinals 4–3 on September 15?
8. Which opposing pitcher threw a no-hitter against the Mets on September 20?
9. How many games back were the Mets of the Chicago Cubs in the National League East on August 13?
10. What was the Mets' record in September?
11. What was the Mets' record at the end of the regular season?
12. Which three players represented the team in the All-Star Game?
13. Who was the team's home run champion?
14. Who led the Mets in RBI?
15. Who had the most hits?
16. In which major offensive category (walks, batting average, hits, doubles, triples, home runs, RBI, runs, on-base percentage, slugging percentage, stolen bases) did the Mets lead the National League?
17. Tom Seaver (25–7) and Gary Gentry (13–12) both made 35 starts. Who gave up more home runs and walks?
18. Who led the team in saves?
19. Who did the Mets beat on September 24 to clinch the division title?
20. Who dubbed the team "The Amazin' Mets?"

Answers

1. 73–89
2. Ninth
3. April. They went 9–11.
4. Nine games
5. 18–23
6. The Houston Astros
7. They were the first major league team to strike out 19 times in a nine-inning game, which they won, 4–3. Ron Swoboda hit a pair of two-run home runs against the Cardinals' Steve Carlton.
8. Bob Moose of the Pittsburgh Pirates
9. 9½
10. 23–7. They won 14 of their last 17 games, and 24 of the final 32.
11. 100–62
12. Cleon Jones, Jerry Koosman, and Tom Seaver
13. Tommie Agee with 26 home runs
14. Tommie Agee with 76 RBIs
15. Cleon Jones with 164 hits. He batted .340.
16. None of them.
17. They both gave up 24 home runs, and Seaver gave up one more walk. He also pitched 40 more innings than Gentry.
18. Ron Taylor with 13, one more than Tug McGraw.
19. The St. Louis Cardinals, 6–0. Gary Gentry threw a four-hitter.
20. Former manager Casey Stengel

Fourteen

The Postseason

 1969

1. Who did the Mets meet in the best-of-five National League Championship Series and what was the result?
2. Who was the winning pitcher in the opener?
3. Who was the losing pitcher?
4. Who hit two-run home runs in Game 2 to pace an 11–6 victory?
5. Who hit the two-run home run in the bottom of the fifth to put the Mets ahead for good in Game 3?
6. Who got the win in relief?
7. Who hit a home run in each game of the series?
8. Who hit a leadoff home run in Game 1 of the World Series?
9. Which team won Game 1 of the World Series?
10. Which three Mets strung together two-out hits to give the Mets a 2–1 lead in the ninth inning of Game 2?
11. Who made the final out of Game 2, and who was the pitcher?
12. Who gave up the only leadoff home run of his career in Game 3, and who hit it?
13. Who made two outstanding catches in the outfield, one a running backhanded catch and the other sprawling at the warning track?

14. Which two pitchers combined for the shutout in the 5–0 victory?
15. Who made the defensive gem to prevent an Orioles rally in Game 4?
16. Who scored the winning run in the 10th inning and why did the Orioles argue the play?
17. Who hit home runs for the Mets in Game 5, and who knocked in what would be the game-winning run?
18. Who allowed just five hits and three runs while throwing a complete game to get the win?
19. Who made the catch for the final out?
20. Who did the Baseball Writers Association of America select as the Series MVP?

(From left) Bud Harrelson looks on as New York mayor John Lindsay holds the champagne to celebrate the Amazin' Mets 1969 World Series victory with annnouncer Lindsay Nelson, Ron Swoboda, and Rod Gasper.

Answers

1. The Mets swept the Braves in three games.
2. Tom Seaver despite allowing five runs over seven innings.
3. Joe Niekro.
4. Tommie Agee, Ken Boswell, and Cleon Jones
5. Wayne Garrett
6. Nolan Ryan
7. Hank Aaron
8. Don Buford off Tom Seaver.
9. The heavily favored Baltimore Orioles, 4–1. It was the only postseason loss for the Mets.
10. Ed Charles, Jerry Grote, and Al Weis
11. After Jerry Koosman pitched 8⅔ innings, Ron Taylor retired Brooks Robinson for the final out.
12. Jim Palmer and Tommie Agee
13. Tommie Agee
14. Gary Gentry threw eight scoreless innings and Nolan Ryan earned the save.
15. Ron Swoboda
16. With two out and no outs pinch-hitter J.C. Martin dropped a bunt and Orioles' pitcher Pete Richert fielded the ball, only to have his throw deflect off Martin into right field. After Rod Gasper scored from second Baltimore argued that Martin was outside the base-path and should have been ruled out.
17. Al Weis and Donn Clendenon hit the home runs while Ron Swoboda knocked in the game-winning run with a double.
18. Jerry Koosman
19. Cleon Jones, a fly ball off the bat of Davey Johnson. Jones gave the ball to Jerry Koosman, who for years stored it in a safe but sold it in the early 1990s.
20. Weis, who batted .455 in the series.

1973

1. On August 5th what place were the New York Mets in the National League East?
2. When did the Mets take over first place?
3. Who did Willie Mays hit his 600th home run off of on August 17th?
4. Which team finished second behind the Mets in the standings?
5. How many players hit .300 or better during the regular season?
6. Who did the Mets beat in the National League Championship Series?
7. What NLCS record did Tom Seaver set in Game 1?
8. Who threw a two-hitter in Game 2?
9. Which two players got into a fight to spark a bench-clearing brawl in Game 3?
10. Who hit two home runs to score four of the Mets runs in the 9–2 victory in Game 3?
11. Who hit a 12th-inning home run in Game 4?
12. Who got the win, giving up only one earned run in 8⅓ innings in Game 5?
13. Whose error led to two unearned runs in the third inning as Oakland took Game 1 of the World Series, 2–1?
14. Who singled in the winning run in the 12th inning of Game 2 for his last hit of his career?
15. Who hit a home run to give the Mets a 2–0 lead in the first inning, only to see the Athletics come back and win in 11 innings 3–2?
16. Who knocked in five runs, with a three-run home run in the first inning and a two-run single in the fourth for the Mets?
17. Who combined for a three-hitter in Game 5?
18. Who hit two RBI doubles off Tom Seaver as the Athletics held off elimination in Game 6?
19. Who, while making his third start in the series, was the losing pitcher in Game 7?
20. Who was named the World Series MVP?

Answers

1. Last
2. September 21 after a 10–2 victory over the Pittsburgh Pirates.
3. Don Gullet of the Cincinnati Reds. The Mets lost 2–1 and were 7½ games back in the standings.
4. The St. Louis Cardinals at 81–81
5. None
6. The Cincinnati Reds as the five-game series went the distance.
7. 13 strikeouts. However, Pete Rose and Johnny Bench hit home runs to lead a 2–1 victory.
8. Jon Matlack
9. Pete Rose and Bud Harrelson. Rose slid in hard into second base to try to break up a double play, to which Harrelson took exception.
10. Rusty Staub
11. Pete Rose
12. Tom Seaver despite walking five and striking out four.
13. Second baseman Félix Millan
14. Willie Mays
15. Wayne Garrett
16. Rusty Staub
17. Jerry Koosman and Tug McGraw
18. Reggie Jackson
19. Jon Matlack
20. Reggie Jackson

1986

1. Who did the Mets play in the National League Championship Series and what was the result?
2. Who threw a five-hitter to win Game 1, and a three-hitter in Game 4?
3. Who scattered 10 hits but gave up only one run to win Game 2?
4. Which two players hit big home runs to lead the Mets' comeback in Game 3?
5. Although neither factored in the decision, which two legendary pitchers faced off in Game 5?
6. Who knocked in the game-winning run with a single in the 12th inning?
7. How many innings did Game 6 go?
8. Down 3–0 in the ninth inning, which three Mets knocked in runs?
9. Who gave up three runs in extra innings, but struck out Kevin Bass with the winning run on base to become the first pitcher to earn three wins in one league championship series?
10. Who committed the error that resulted in the only run in Game 1 of the World Series?
11. Who gave up eight hits and six runs (five earned) in five innings as Boston won 9–3 behind 18 hits in Game 2?
12. Who hit a leadoff home run to spark a four-run rally in the first inning that held up in Game 3?
13. Who threw seven scoreless innings to help the Mets tie the series with a 6–2 victory?
14. Who earned a complete-game victory in Game 5 to send the series back to New York with Boston leading 3–2?
15. Down 2–0 in the fifth inning whose key RBI-single helped tie the game?
16. Down 3–2 in the eighth inning, whose sacrifice fly again tied the score?
17. Who hit what initially appeared to be the death blow to the Mets, a 10th-inning home run?

October 26, 1986: Ray Knight raises his arms after hitting a home run in Game 7 of the 1986 World Series. (Richard Drew)

18. Down 5–3, who started the Mets' famous rally in the bottom of the 10th inning?

19. Who came into the game and threw a wild pitch that tied the score?

20. Who was the batter to hit the ground ball that went through Bill Buckner's legs?

21. Who scored the dramatic winning run?

22. Who was the winning pitcher of Game 6?

23. Who was the winning pitcher of Game 7?

24. Who had three hits including a home run in Game 7 and was named World Series MVP?

25. Who did a lot of people think should get the award after having nine RBIs in the Series and hitting two home runs over the Green Monster (both in Game 4)?

Answers

1. The Houston Astros. The Mets won in six games.
2. Astros ace Mike Scott, who would have started Game 7 as well.
3. Bobby Ojeda
4. Darryl Strawberry hit a three-run home run and Lenny Dykstra had a two-run home run to pace the 6–5 victory.
5. Nolan Ryan and Dwight Gooden. Ryan gave up just two hits over nine innings and struck out 12 while walking just one. Gooden allowed nine over 10 innings, but both left the game when the score was 1–1.
6. Gary Carter
7. 16. It lasted four hours and 42 minutes.
8. Mookie Wilson, Keith Hernandez, and Ray Knight
9. Reliever Jesse Orosco
10. Second baseman Tim Teufel
11. Dwight Gooden
12. Lenny Dykstra
13. Ron Darling
14. Bruce Hurst. He was also the winning pitcher in Game 1.
15. Ray Knight
16. Gary Carter
17. Dave Henderson
18. Gary Carter, with Kevin Mitchell, and Ray Knight following with base hits off Calvin Schiraldi to score Carter and bring the deficit to 5–4.
19. Bob Stanley on a 2–2 count. The Red Sox were one pitch away from winning the World Series when it occurred.
20. Mookie Wilson
21. Ray Knight
22. Rick Aguilera, who had given up the home run to Henderson.
23. Roger McDowell
24. Ray Knight
25. Gary Carter

 **1988**

1. How many games did the Mets win during the regular season?
2. How many of those wins came against the Dodgers out of 11 games?
3. Who led the National League with 39 home runs and drove in 101 runs during the regular season?
4. Which two Mets hit run-scoring doubles in the ninth inning to lead a 3–2 victory in Game 1?
5. Who did the Dodgers score five runs against during the first two innings of Game 2 en route to a 6–3 victory?
6. Who had the game-tying double, and the single to give the Mets the lead with two outs in the eighth inning as part of a five-run rally in Game 3?
7. Who hit the series-turning two-run home run off Dwight Gooden in the ninth inning of Game 4?
8. Who hit the game-winning home run in the 12th inning?
9. Two players in particular led the 5–1 victory in Game 6. Who went 4-for-4 at the plate, and who earned the complete-game win?
10. Who threw a five-hitter in Game 7 to end the Mets' season?

1999

1.   Despite winning 97 games during the regular season, who did the Mets have to beat to get into the playoffs?

2.   Who threw a two-hitter in the winner-takes-all game?

3.   Who did the Mets play in a Divisional Series and what was the result?

4.   Who hit two home runs in Game 1, including a grand slam in the ninth inning to lead an 8–4 victory?

5.   Why did a lot of Mets fans not see the grand slam live on television?

6.   Who knocked in five runs to lead a 7–1 victory in Game 2?

7.   Who was sidelined for Game 3, a 9–2 victory for the Mets, with a bad thumb?

8.   Who ended the series with a dramatic home run in the 10th inning?

9.   Who would have started Game 5 for the Diamondbacks had the series gone that far?

10. Who did the Mets face in the National League Championship Series and what was the outcome?

11. Who did the Mets start in Game 1 against Greg Maddux?

12. Which two players hit two-run home runs to lead a 4–3 victory in Game 2?

13. Neither starting pitcher gave up an earned run Game 3. What was the pitching matchup and how was the game decided?

14. Who hit a home run in the sixth inning and a two-run single in the eighth inning to lead the 3–2 victory in Game 4?

15. How did the Braves take a 3–2 lead in the 15th inning of Game 5?

16. Who singled to center after a 12-pitch at-bat to lead off the 15th for the Mets?

17. Who drew a bases-loaded walk to tie the game?

18. Who hit the dramatic grand slam to win the game?

19. How was it officially scored and why?

20. Who gave up five runs in the first inning, who threw four scoreless innings to give the Mets a chance to come back, and who ended up walking in the decisive run in the 11th inning to take the loss?

Answers

1. In a one-game playoff at Cincinnati with the National League wild-card spot on the line the Mets beat the Reds 2–0.
2. Al Leiter
3. The Mets faced the Arizona Diamondbacks and won in four games.
4. Edgardo Alfonzo
5. Television gave Diamondbacks owner Jerry Colangelo the option of playing the game on a weekday afternoon or late in the evening. Because it was the franchise's first playoff game ever he opted for the night game to convenience the hometown fans. Factor in the time zones and Alfonzo's grand slam occurred well after midnight in New York.
6. Steve Finley
7. Mike Piazza
8. Backup catch Todd Pratt
9. Cy Young Award winner Randy Johnson.
10. The Atlanta Braves, who won the series in six games.
11. Masato Yoshii, who took the loss.
12. Brian Jordan and Eddie Perez
13. Tom Glavine vs. Al Leiter. Two errors in the first inning led to a run and with the 1–0 victory the Braves led the series 3–0.
14. John Olerud
15. Keith Lockhart's triple off Octavio Dotel scored Walt Weiss.
16. Shawon Dunston
17. Todd Pratt
18. Robin Ventura
19. Ventura was mobbed by teammates and never touched home plate. It's officially scored as a single, but called by fans the "grand-slam single."
20. Al Leiter started, Pat Mahomes relieved him in the first inning, and Kenny Rogers took the loss. The bullpen was spent after nine pitchers participated in Game 5, and eight were used in Game 6.

2000

1. What franchise first did the Mets do by winning 94 games during the regular season?
2. What did a lot of players credit for pulling the team together early on?
3. Who did the Mets face in a National League Division Series and what was the outcome?
4. Who hit the home run in Game 1 to lead a 5–1 victory?
5. Who did John Franco strike out for the final out in the 5–4 victory in Game 2?
6. Which reserve player had three hits and two RBIs, and who knocked in the winning run with a 10th inning single?
7. Who hit the game-winning home run in the 13th inning of Game 3?
8. Who threw the first postseason one-hitter in 33 years during Game 4?
9. Who did the Mets in play in the National League Championship Series and what was the result?
10. Who threw seven scoreless innings to get the win in Game 1?
11. After the Mets saw three leads evaporate in Game 2, who knocked in the winning run with a ninth-inning single?
12. Which starting pitcher gave up six hits and two runs over eight innings to get the win in Game 3?
13. Against which starting pitcher did the Mets set a postseason record with five doubles in one inning (the first) in Game 4?
14. Who threw a three-hitter to close out the series?
15. Who set an NLCS record by scoring eight runs during the series?
16. Whose bases-loaded two-out single in the 12th inning decided Game 1 of the World Series?
17. What was Roger Clemens fined $50,000 for doing during Game 2?
18. Who snapped a 2–2 tie with an RBI double in the eighth inning of Game 3, and who had a two-run home run in Game 4?

19. Whose ninth-inning, two-out, RBI-single to center field broke a 2–2 tie in Game 6 and essentially locked up the championship?
20. Combined, how many teams finished better in the regular season standings than the Yankees and Mets?

Umpire Charlie Reliford gets between Mike Piazza and Roger Clemens during the broken bat incident in the first inning of Game 2 of the 2000 World Series. (Ron Frehm)

Answers

1. The Mets qualified for the postseason in consecutive seasons for the first time.
2. Opening the season in Tokyo, Japan.
3. The Mets beat the San Francisco Giants in four games.
4. Ellis Burks
5. Barry Bonds
6. Timo Perez and Jay Payton
7. Benny Agbayani
8. Bobby J. Jones
9. The Mets beat the St. Louis Cardinals in five games.
10. Mike Hampton
11. Jay Payton
12. Andy Benes
13. Darryl Kile
14. Mike Hampton, who was named the series MVP.
15. Timo Perez
16. Jose Vizcaino
17. He threw the jagged barrel of a shattered bat toward Mike Piazza. He was not ejected and pitched eight shutout innings. Despite scoring five runs in the ninth inning, on a two-run home run by Piazza and a three-run blast by Jay Payton, the Mets fell short, 6–5.
18. Benny Agbayani and Mike Piazza
19. Luis Sojo
20. Seven

2006

1. Who did the Mets face in a National League Division Series and what was the result?

2. What did Carlos Delgado become just the fifth player in Major League history to do in Game 1?

3. What unusual defensive play in the second inning of Game 1 helped set the tone for the series?

4. Who recorded the 13th postseason win of his career in Game 2?

5. Who had three hits, two RBIs and caught the final out as the Mets defeated his former team 9–5 in Game 3?

6. Who did the Mets face in the National League Championship Series and what was the result?

7. Which three Mets pitchers combined for a 2–0 shutout in Game 1?

8. Who hit two home runs and drove in four runs for the Mets in Game 2?

9. Who pitched eight scoreless innings in Game 3?

10. Who hit two home runs in Game 4 to help lead a 12–5 victory?

11. Who gave up home runs to Albert Pujols and Chris Duncan while taking the loss in Gave 5?

12. Who led off Game 6 with a home run?

13. Who leapt high above the top of the left-field wall to rob Scott Rolen of a two-run home run in the sixth inning of Game 7?

14. Who hit the crucial two-run home run in the ninth inning to break a 1–1 tie?

15. Who did he hit it off of?

Answers

1. The Mets swept the Dodgers in three games.
2. Have four or more hits with at least one home run in his first career postseason game. The four hits also tied a franchise postseason record.
3. Catcher Paul Lo Duca tagged out two Dodgers at home plate on the same play. Specifically, off Russell Martin's single to right, Shawn Green retrieved the ball and threw it to second baseman Jose Valentin, whose relay throw to Lo Duca was in time for the catcher to not only tag out Jeff Kent at the plate, but J.D. Drew trying to score as well. The Mets won 4–1.
4. Tom Glavine
5. Shawn Green
6. The St. Louis Cardinals won in seven games.
7. Tom Glavine, Guillermo Mota, and Billy Wagner
8. Carlos Delgado, but the Mets still lost 9–6.
9. Jeff Suppan
10. Carlos Beltran, while Carlos Delgado have five RBIs.
11. Tom Glavine
12. Jose Reyes
13. Endy Chavez
14. Yadier Molina
15. Aaron Heilman

2015

1. Why were the number of innings starter Matt Harvey pitched during the regular season a cause for concern?
2. What major acquisition did the Mets add near the trading deadline?
3. Who teared up on the field after he thought he had been traded, only to hit a game-winning home run against Washington two nights later?
4. Who was manager Terry Collins talking about when he said down the stretch: "We'd like to open up here. It beats facing those two animals out there in the shadows. That's not very much fun."
5. Who opened the playoffs by striking out 13 batters over seven scoreless innings?
6. Who broke shortstop Ruben Tejada's right leg in a takeout slide during Game 2, infuriating the Mets?
7. During Game 3, who knocked in five runs to tie a Mets postseason record? (Bonus: Whose record did he tie?)
8. Who on three days rest struck out eight, walked one, and yielded only three hits over seven innings to tie up the series?
9. Who stole an uncovered third base, scored the tying run, and then hit a go-ahead home run to lead the Mets to a 3–2 victory in Game 5?
10. Who gave up four hits while striking out nine batters over 7⅔ innings to get the win in Game 1 of the National League Championship Series?
11. In Game 2 who gave up his first first-inning run in 25 consecutive starts dating back to May 29?
12. Who hit his fifth postseason home run in the first inning of Game 3?
13. In Game 4 who set a record by hitting a home run in his sixth consecutive postseason game?
14. Who set a Major League record for longest amount of time between postseason victories?

15. What was the Mets' record against the Cubs during the regular season?
16. Who led off the World Series with an inside-the-park home run, and more than five hours later scored the winning run in the 14th inning?
17. Who threw a two-hitter in Game 2?
18. Who hit a home run in his first World Series at-bat at Citi Field, and drove in four runs in Game 3?
19. Who made an error in the three-run eighth inning in Game 4 that put the Mets on the brink of elimination?
20. Who, when his manager tried to pull him after throwing eight scoreless innings, said "No way" in Game 5?

Noah Syndergaard, Matt Harvey, and Jacob deGrom walk Citi Field before a game against the Cardinals. (Icon Sportswire)

Answers

1. Matt Harvey missed the 2014 season following Tommy John elbow surgery and his agent went out of his way to announce that he should be shut down after pitching 180 innings.
2. Yoenis Cespedes
3. Wilmer Flores
4. Clayton Kershaw and Zack Greinke, whom he didn't want to face in the afternoon at Dodger Stadium. However, the Mets still didn't win home field advantage for the National League Division Series.
5. Jacob deGrom
6. Chase Utley
7. Curtis Granderson with two doubles off the wall at Citi Field. He tied the record set by Carlos Delgado in Game 4 of the 2006 NLCS at St. Louis.
8. Clayton Kershaw
9. Daniel Murphy
10. Matt Harvey
11. Jake Arrieta of the Chicago Cubs
12. Kyle Schwarber
13. Daniel Murphy, who said afterwards, "I can't explain what I'm doing." He batted .529 (9-for-17) in the series to be named the NLCS MVP.
14. 42-year-old pitcher Bartolo Colon recorded his first postseason win since 2001. According to STATS it had been 14 years, 12 days between postseason victories for Colon, topping the previous record of exactly 14 years by Milt Wilcox.
15. 0–7
16. Alcides Escobar of the Kansas City Royals, who won Game 1, 5–4. He scored the winning run on Eric Hosmer's sacrifice fly.
17. Johnny Cueto
18. David Wright
19. Second baseman Daniel Murphy
20. Matt Harvey. He gave up two runs in the ninth, and after the game went into extra innings the Royals scored five runs in the 12th inning to win the World Series. The Royals came back from a deficit in all four wins.

Fifteen

Miscellaneous

From the stadiums to World Series and the Hall of Famers, just about every aspect of the New York Mets has been covered, right?
Hardly.

This section will test your knowledge of the Mets oddities and eccentricities. From the odd moments to the unusual statistics that just don't quite fit in anywhere else.

 Miscellaneous

1. Through 2015 the Mets have only had four team captains in their illustrious history. Name them.
2. What unusual "double" have relievers Craig Anderson, Willard Hunter, and Jesse Orosco all done for the Mets?
3. Which two players hit grand slams when the Mets scored 11 runs in the sixth inning at Wrigley Field on July 16, 2006?
4. Who was the first general manager in Mets history?
5. Who held the general manager position the longest?
6. Who retired having recorded 35 wins against the Mets, the most of any pitcher?

7. In 2009 Kelvim Escobar became the fifth pitcher to collect 100 wins and 50 saves over a career. Name the other four.

8. Who tied a National League record by drawing a walk to reach base in 15 straight at-bats?

9. What Mets pitcher hit two home runs at Chicago on August 6, 1983?

10. Between Tug McGraw, Nolan Ryan, Tom Seaver, Jerry Koosman, Jon Matlack, Ron Darling, Dwight Gooden, David Cone, and Pedro Martinez, only one gave up a hit to the first batter he faced as a Met. Who was it and who was the batter?

11. Who hit the 6,000th home run in franchise history on September 13, 2009, at Citizens Bank Park in Philadelphia?

12. Who leads the Mets in all-time pinch-hit home runs?

13. Who are the only two pitchers in Mets history to strike out the side on nine pitches?

14. In 2008 Johan Santana became the sixth pitcher to make his Mets debut as the starting pitcher on Opening Day. Name them and which one among them didn't lose.

15. Name the first player to hit three home runs in a game against the Mets, and the first player to do it twice.

16. The Mets' media guide lists the 10-game road trip from August 9–18, 1991, as the worst in franchise history as the team failed to notch a victory. What three teams were visited?

17. What team did the Mets come back from an eight-run deficit to defeat 11–8 on September 2, 1972?

18. What very unusual combination did Nelson Figueroa pull off as a relief pitcher against the St. Louis Cardinals on August 5, 2009?

19. What's the most saves recorded by a pitcher during his first season with the Mets?

20. Who is listed last on the Mets' all-time alphabetical roster?

21. In 1996 the Mets wore a special logo honoring whom?

22. Who hit the first home run in a Mets uniform during an All-Star Game?

23. Who is the only Mets player to lead the National League in stolen bases?
24. Who hit grand slams in both games of a doubleheader on May 20, 1999?
25. Who hit his 400th home run on August 22, 2006?
26. Who notched career victory No. 300 on August 5, 2007?
27. Who was the winning pitcher of both a 19-inning game and an 18-inning game during the 1985 season?
28. Who was the winning pitcher on Opening Day in 1985 when Gary Carter hit a walk-off home run in his first Mets game?
29. The Mets' attendance record for a home game is 57,175. Name the stadium and opponent when it was set.
30. After losing 13 straight times who did the Mets finally beat on August 26, 1965?
31. What historical doubleheader did the Mets play in on July 8, 2000?
32. Who had the only six-hit game in Mets history?
33. When Shawn Green retired after the 2007 season, he was second in career home runs and RBIs and 10th in batting average among all-time Jewish players. Who led those categories?
34. Balance was a theme of the 2000 team and seven different players reached double figures in home runs. Name them.
35. After the Mets clinched the 2015 National League Eastern Division, who called manager Terry Collins in the clubhouse to offer congratulations?
36. When the Mets traded for Yoenis Cespedes in 2015, who tweeted: "I can't believe I can actually say this, but is it true that there is now 'a Cespedes for the rest of us'"?
37. Who did Tom Seaver strike out to become the first pitcher in Major League history to record 200-plus strikeouts for the eighth consecutive year?
38. Who has the fewest wins as a manager for the Mets?
39. Through 2009, the Mets had a winning record on only one holiday. Which one was it?
40. Who wrote the *Meet the Mets* theme song in 1962?

Answers

1. Keith Hernandez 1987–1989, Gary Carter 1988–1989, John Franco 2001–2004, David Wright 2013–15
2. They were the winning pitcher in both games of a doubleheader.
3. Cliff Floyd and Carlos Beltran
4. Charlie Weiss in 1962
5. Frank Cashen, who held the position for 11 years (1980–1990).
6. Greg Maddux
7. John Smoltz, Derek Lowe, Tom Gordon, and Dennis Eckersley
8. Jon Olerud in 1999
9. Walt Terrell
10. Tom Seaver, a double to Matty Alou of the Pittsburgh Pirates on April 13, 1967.
11. Anderson Hernandez
12. Mark Carreon with eight.
13. Nolan Ryan and David Cone. Ryan did it in the third inning on April 19, 1968, vs. Los Angeles (Claude Osteen, Wes Parker, and Zoilo Versalles). Cone did it in the fifth inning, August 30, 1991, at Cincinnati (Herm Winningham, Randy Myers, and Mariano Duncan).
14. Roger Craig (1962), Don Cardwell (1967), Mike Hampton (2000), Tom Glavine (2003), and Pedro Martinez (2005). Only Martinez didn't lose.
15. Stan Musial was the first player on July 8. 1962. And as of this publication, Willie McCovey was the only player to hit three home runs during a game twice against the Mets on September 22, 1963 and September 17, 1966. Both games were played in San Francisco.
16. The Cubs, Cardinals, and Pirates
17. The Astros
18. He got the win and hit a triple. He was the first pitcher to do that since 1972 (Jim Colborn).
19. Billy Wagner with 40 saves in 2006.
20. Don Zimmer, who played third base in 1962.
21. John McSherry, an umpire who died during a game on Opening Day of the 1996 season.
22. Lee Mazzilli in 1979.
23. Jose Reyes in 2005, 2006, and 2007.
24. Robin Ventura
25. Carlos Delgado
26. Tom Glavine
27. Tom Gorman (according to the Elias Sports Bureau, Ed Reulbach of the Cubs is the only other pitcher in Major League history to win a pair of 18-inning games in a season).
28. Tom Gorman. He apparently predicted that he would win the game beforehand, to which manager Davey Johnson replied: "You won't even sniff this game."
29. It was a doubleheader against the Los Angeles Dodgers at Shea Stadium on June 13, 1965.
30. Sandy Koufax
31. The Mets and Yankees played in the first day-night doubleheader at different venues since 1903. The first game was played at Shea Stadium, the second at Yankee Stadium. The Yankees won both 4–2.
32. Edgardo Alfonzo at Houston on August 30, 1999. He was 6-for-6 with three home runs.

33. Hank Greenberg led in home runs and RBIs, while Morrie Arnovich had the best batting average.
34. Mike Piazza (38), Edgardo Alfonzo (25), Robin Ventura (24), Todd Zeile (22), Derek Bell (18), Jay Payton (17) and Benny Agbayani (15).
35. His friend Sandy Koufax. The Mets and Dodgers were set to play in a National League Division Series.
36. Jerry Seinfeld (if you don't get it, look it up)
37. Manny Sanguillen of the Pittsburgh Pirates in 1975.
38. Mike Cubbage with three in 1991.
39. Mother's Day. It had a losing record on Easter, Memorial Day, Father's Day, Independence Day. and Labor Day.
40. Ruth Roberts and Bill Katz

Sixteen

The Hot Box

We'll ease you into this.

During the 1973 World Series the New York Mets faced the colorful Oakland Athletics, whose clashing personalities were about as dull as the team's bright uniforms (in other words, not at all).

While owner Charles O. Finley and hitters like American League MVP Reggie Jackson drew a lot of attention, the matchup featured the reigning champions against the team with the worst record to ever play in a World Series (82–79).

Nevertheless, here are seven questions regarding the seven-game series:

What rule was in effect for the first time in a World Series?

Who won Games 1 and 7 for the A's?

Which A's reliever was the losing pitcher in Game 2?

Who pitched in all seven games for the A's and notched two saves?

Who got outpitched by Jerry Koosman in Game 5?

Who outdueled Tom Seaver in Game 6?

Who quit his job after the Series concluded?

The answers are: the designated hitter, Ken Holtzman (21–3 in the regular season), Rollie Fingers, Darold Knowles, Vida Blue (20–9), Catfish Hunter (21–5), and Oakland manager Dick Williams.

Each of the following questions is like those seven combined.

When it comes to New York Mets trivia, these are some of the hardest of the hard, the ones that even the staunchest fans will struggle with and say: "Are you kidding me?"

 # The Hot Box

1. On August 17, 2002, the All-Amazin' Team was announced in celebration of the Mets' 40th anniversary. Name the 15 people who were selected by fans.
2. Who were the first 10 players to play 10 years for the Mets?
3. Casey Stengel's final game as a manager was on July 24, 1965. Name the opponent, final score, winning pitcher, losing pitcher, and who had the only hits for the Mets.
4. Who holds the record for games played for the Mets at each position (pitcher not included, list only one outfielder)?
5. When Jason Bay joined the team in 2010 he became the sixth Canadian to play for the Mets. Who were the first five?
6. Which six Mets have perfect batting averages?
7. Before Tom Seaver in 1967, who were the Mets' representatives to the All-Star Game, and which one of them started?
8. Through 2009 eight different Mets had hit home runs from both sides of the plate in one game. Name them.
9. Name the 10 Mets who played for the team as teenagers.
10. Name the first 10 Mets who were born in Japan. (Bonus: Spell their names)
11. Name the people who have had to pronounce their names, along with every other players', the 10 public address announcers through 2015.
12. When Gil Hodges became the second first baseman in Major League history to hit four home runs in a game on August 31, 1950, who were the four pitchers?
13. The 1986 Mets are one of only 11 teams since 1900 to win 108 games during a single season. Name the other 10.

14. List the Mets' single-season home run leaders by position (include each outfield position and pitcher, but not the designated hitter from facing American League foes).

15. Now do the same thing with the Mets' RBI leaders by position.

16. Name the only player in franchise history to have an inside-the-park home run as a pinch-hitter, and the only one to hit one during his second at-bat in an inning.

17. Name the only two Mets pitchers to have hit a grand slam—who were the players on base, and what was the added significance of the first one?

18. Jerry Koosman was one of 54 Major League players who served in the military during the Vietnam War. Name them.

19. Name the players involved the first five times the Mets had two pinch-hitters connect for home runs in the same game.

20. Name the 22 players the Mets acquired in the expansion draft on October 10, 1961.

21. In 2006 the Mets hit 10 grand slams. Who hit them?

22. The Mets have played eight games that resulted in a tie. Name the opponents and the final scores.

23. Mike Piazza is one of 10 players in Major League history to have over 400 home runs with a .300 career average while having never struck out more than 100 times in a season. Name the other nine.

24. As previously mentioned Tom Seaver used to have the highest percentage of induction votes in the history of the Baseball Hall of Fame (now Ken Griffey Jr.). Name the next 14 (which will end with another former New York Met).

25. Name the first 27 inductees into the Mets Hall of Fame (through 2015).

Answers

1. Keith Hernandez 1B; Edgardo Alfonzo 2B; Buddy Harrelson SS; Howard Johnson 3B; Mike Piazza C; Lenny Dykstra OF; Darryl Strawberry OF; Mookie Wilson OF; Tom Seaver RHP; Jerry Koosman LHP; Roger McDowell RHP; John Franco LHP; Ed Kranepool PH; Rusty Staub PH; Gil Hodges Manager.

2. Ed Kranepool (1962–79), Bud Harrelson (1965–77), Jerry Grote (1966–77), Cleon Jones (1963–75), Tom Seaver (1967–79, 1983), Ron Hodges (1973–84), Jerry Koosman (1967–78), Dwight Gooden (1984–94), Mookie Wilson (1980–89), and Lee Mazzilli (1976–81, 1986–89).

3. The Phillies won 5–1. Jim Bunning threw a two-hitter for the win, while Johnny Lewis had the hits, including a home run. Tom Parsons took the loss.

4. C Jerry Grote; 1B Ed Kranepool; 2B Wally Backman; SS Bud Harrelson; 3B David Wright; OF Cleon Jones. The next two on the outfield list are Darryl Strawberry and Mookie Wilson.

5. RHP Ray Daviault, LHP Ken Mackenzie, INF Tim Harkness, RHP Ron Taylor, and INF Brian Ostrosser.

6. Jason Roach 2–2, Eric Cammack 1–1, Gary Bennett 1–1, Ray Searage 1–1, Dave Liddell 1–1, Rodney McCray 1–1.

7. 1962 Richie Ashburn, OF; 1963 Duke Snider, OF; 1964 Ron Hunt, 2B; 1965 Ed Kranepool, 1B; and 1966 Ron Hunt, 2B. Hunt started in 1964 at Shea Stadium and went 1–3 with a single in the third inning off the Angels' Dean Chance.

8. Lee Mazzilli, Howard Johnson, Bobby Bonilla, Todd Hundley, Carl Everett, Tony Clark, Jose Reyes, and Carlos Beltran.

9. Ed Kranepool, Jim Bethke, Jerry Hinsley, Kevin Collins, Dwight Gooden, Nolan Ryan, Greg Goossen, Tim Foli, Jose Oquendo and Jose Reyes.

10. Takashi Kashiwada (1997), Hideo Nomo (1998), Masato Yoshii (1998–1999), Satoru Komiyama (2002), Tsuyoshi Shinjo (2001, 2003), Kazuhisa Ishii (2005), Shingo Takatsu (2005), Kazuo Matsui (2004–2006), Ken Takahashi (2009), and Ryota Igarashi (2010).

11. Jack E. Lee (1962–66), Dan Reilly (1966), Jack Lightcap (1966–70), Loren Matthews (1970–76), Jack Franchetti (1977–87), Pete Larkin (1988–93), Don/Doug Gould (1994), Del DeMontreaux (1995–99), Roger Luce (2000–03), Alex Anthony (2003–15).

12. The home runs in order: In the second inning off Warren Spahn, the third inning off Normie Roy, the sixth inning off Bob Hall, and finally the eighth inning off Johnny Antonelli.

13. 1906 Cubs, 2001 Mariners, 1998 Yankees, 1954 Indians, 1909 Pirates, 1927 Yankees, 1961 Yankees, 1969 Orioles, 1970 Orioles, and 1975 Reds.

14. C Todd Hundley 41 (1996); 1B Carlos Delgado 38 (2006 & 2008); 2B Edgardo Alfonzo 27 (1999); SS Jose Reyes 19 (2006); 3B Howard Johnson 38 (1991); LF Dave Kingman 26 (1975); CF Carlos Beltran 41 (2006); RF Darryl Strawberry 38 (1987 & 1988); P Tom Seaver 3 (1972) and Walt Terrell 3 (1983)

15. C Mike Piazza 124 (1999); 1B Carlos Delgado 115 (2008); 2B Edgardo Alfonzo 108 (1999); SS Jose Reyes 81 (2006); 3B David Wright 124 (2008); LF Bernard Gilkey 117 (1996); CF Carlos Beltran 116 (2006); RF Darryl Strawberry 108 (1990); P Tom Seaver 10 (1970)

16. Marlon Anderson had the pinch-hit inside-the-park home run against the Angels on June 11, 2005, and Doug Flynn hit his during his second at-bat of an inning against the Reds on June 12, 1979.

17. Carl Willey against Houston on July 15, 1963, with Frank Thomas, Joe Hicks, and Larry Burright on base, which was also the first home run hit by a Mets pitcher; and Jack Hamilton against St. Louis on May 20, 1967, with Tommy Davis, Ken Boyer, and Jerry Grote.

18. Vic Albury, Matt Alexander, Frank Baker, Jim Bibby, Larry Biittner, Gene Brabender, Al Bumbry, Darrel Chaney, Bruce Christensen, Mike Davison, Ed Figueroa, Rich Folkers, Ted Ford, Larry French, Wayne Garrett, Roy Gleason, Chuck Goggin, Dave Goltz, Doug Griffin, Tom Heintzelman, Phil Hennigan, Jim Holt, Mike Jackson, Ray Jarvis, Bob Johnson, Bob Jones, Jerry Kenney, Jim Kern, Jerry Koosman, John Lowenstein, Garry Maddox, Jim Magnuson, Gene Martin, Larry Miller, George Mitterwald, Curt Motton, Thurman Munson, Bobby Murcer, Ray Newman, Scott Northey, Darrell Osteen, Harry Parker, Hal Quick, Dave Schneck, Mickey Scott, Rich Severson, Fred Stanley, Leroy Stanton, Earl Stephenson, Jim Strickland, Champ Summers, Jerry Terrell, Floyd Wicker, George Zeber. Source: Baseball Almanac.

19. Choo Choo Coleman and Jim Hickman against the Phillies in 1962, Joe Hicks and Frank Thomas vs. the Phillies in 1963, John Stephenson and Ron Swoboda against the Giants in 1966, Mackey Sasser and Mark Carreon vs. the Giants in 1991, and Butch Huskey and Carl Everett against the Cardinals in 1997.

20. Pitchers: Jay Hook (Cincinnati), Bob L. Miller (St. Louis); Craig Anderson (St. Louis), Roger Craig (Los Angeles), Ray Daviault (San Francisco), Al Jackson (Pittsburgh); Sherman Jones (Cincinnati).
Catchers: Chris Cannizzaro (St. Louis), Clarence Coleman (Philadelphia), Hobie Landrith (San Francisco).
Infielders: Don Zimmer (Chicago); Ed Bouchee (Chicago), Elio Chacon (Cincinnati), Sammy Drake (Chicago), Gil Hodges (Los Angeles) Felix Mantilla (Milwaukee).
Outfielders: Lee Walls (Philadelphia); Gus Bell (Cincinnati), Joe Christopher (Pittsburgh), John DeMerit (Milwaukee); Bobby Gene Smith (Philadelphia); Jim Hickman (St. Louis).

21. Carlos Beltran with three, Jose Valentin with two, David Wright with two, Cliff Floyd, Jose Reyes and Carlos Deldago all with one.

22. September 9, 1962: 7–7 vs. Colt 45's at Houston
June 7, 1964 (Game 2): 1–1 vs. Dodgers at Shea Stadium
May 31, 1965 (Game 2): 3–3 vs. Cubs at Chicago
October 2, 1965 (Game 2): 0–0 vs. Phillies at Shea Stadium (18 innings)
September 2, 1968 (Game 2): 2–2 vs. Braves at Shea Stadium
May 25, 1979: 3–3 vs. Pirates at Shea Stadium (11 innings)
April 22, 1981: 2–2 vs. Pirates at Pittsburgh
October 1, 1981: 2–2 vs. Cubs at Shea Stadium

23. Ted Williams, Stan Musial, Lou Gehrig, Mel Ott, Hank Aaron, Babe Ruth, Vladimir Guerrero, Albert Pujols and Chipper Jones.

24. The next 14, with year, votes and percentage included:
Nolan Ryan, 1999, 497, 491, 98.79%
Cal Ripken, Jr., 2007, 545, 537, 98.53%
Ty Cobb, 1936, 226, 222, 98.23%
George Brett, 1999, 497, 488, 98.19%
Hank Aaron, 1982, 415, 406, 97.83%

Tony Gwynn, 2007, 545, 532, 97.61%
Greg Maddux, 2014, 571, 555, 97.20%
Mike Schmidt, 1995, 460, 444, 96.52%
Johnny Bench, 1989, 447, 431, 96.42%
Steve Carlton, 1994, 455, 436, 95.82%
Babe Ruth, 1936, 226, 215, 95.13%
Honus Wagner, 1936, 226, 215, 95.13%
Rickey Henderson, 2009, 539, 511, 94.81%
Willie Mays, 1979, 432, 409, 94.68%
25. In alphabetical order and the year inducted:
Tommie Agee 2002
Gary Carter 2001
Frank Cashen 2010
John Franco 2012
Dwight Gooden 2010
Jerry Grote 1992
Bud Harrelson 1986
Keith Hernandez 1997
Gil Hodges 1982
Davey Johnson 2010
Cleon Jones 1991
Ralph Kiner 1984
Jerry Koosman 1989
Ed Kranepool 1990
Tug McGraw 1993
Bob Murphy 1984
Johnny Murphy 1983
Lindsey Nelson 1984
Joan Payson 1981
Mike Piazza 2013
Tom Seaver 1988
Bill Shea 1983
Rusty Staub 1986
Casey Stengel 1981
Darryl Strawberry 2010
Mookie Wilson 1996
George Weiss 1982

About the Author

Christopher Walsh has been an award-winning sportswriter since 1990 and has authored 24 books. He's been twice nominated for a Pulitzer Prize, won three Football Writers Association of America awards, and received both the 2006 and 2014 Herby Kirby Memorial Award, the Alabama Sports Writers Association's highest honor for story of the year. Originally from Minnesota and a graduate of the University of New Hampshire, he currently works for Bleacher Report and resides in Tuscaloosa, Alabama.

His other books include:

Sweet 16: Alabama's Historic 2015 Championship Season, 2016

Cubs Triviology, 2016

Mets Triviology, 2016

Nick Saban vs. College Football, 2014.

100 Things Crimson Tide Fans Need to Know & Do Before They Die, 2008; updated 2012

Cowboys Triviology, 2011

Packers Triviology, 2011

Steelers Triviology, 2011

Huddle Up: New York Giants Football, 2009.

Huddle Up: Alabama Football, 2009.

Huddle Up: Michigan Football, 2009.

Huddle Up: Notre Dame Football, 2009.

Huddle Up: Ohio State Football, 2009.

Huddle Up: Oklahoma Football, 2009.

Huddle Up: Tennessee Football, 2009.

Huddle Up: Texas Football, 2009.

Who's No. 1? 100-Plus Years of Controversial Champions in College Football, 2007.

Where Football is King: A History of the SEC, 2006.

No Time Outs: What It's Really Like to be a Sportswriter Today, 2006.

Crimson Storm Surge: Alabama Football, Then and Now, 2005.

Return to Glory: The Story of Alabama's 2008 Season, 2009 (contributing writer).